NEVER

LOOK

DOWN

NEVER
LOOK
DOWN

HOW FREE CLIMBING CHANGED MY LIFE

JAMES KINGSTON

WITH IAN PREECE

BLINK

bringing you closer

Published by Blink Publishing
3.25, The Plaza,
535 Kings Road,
Chelsea Harbour,
London, SW10 0SZ

www.blinkpublishing.co.uk

facebook.com/blinkpublishing
twitter.com/blinkpublishing

Hardback – 978-1-911274-38-4
Ebook – 978-1-911274-43-8

Design by www.envydesignltd.co.uk
Printed and bound in Italy

1 3 5 7 9 10 8 6 4 2

Papers used by Blink Publishing are natural, recyclable products made
from wood grown in sustainable forests. The manufacturing processes
conform to the environmental regulations of the country of origin.

Blink Publishing is an imprint of the Bonnier Publishing Group
www.bonnierpublishing.co.uk

CONTENTS

MORETON, BIRKEN-HEAD, THE WIRRAL

INTRODUCTION

IF YOU FALL EITHER WAY, YOU'RE GONE

It was pitch-black and it was cold – still winter-time, February or March 2013. I could jump between rooftops pretty easily by then – I knew my feet would land safely. With leaps between roofs, once you've taken off, you know you can't fail. But high up a huge crane, you're essentially balanced on a little railing – if you fall either way, you're gone. But this particular night opened my eyes to something else.

I've got some really good parkour friends up on Merseyside, in Moreton, on the Wirral. My friend Danny and his brother Stevy live up there. Danny was bored one night and said, 'Oh, let's just go for a drive.' Before long we came across this crane, out somewhere towards Birkenhead. It turned out he'd already done it – so it was no surprise when he parked the car and said, 'Yeah, let's go up this crane.'

The climb was pretty easy for someone used to going up drainpipes – physically, it was super-easy. Basically, the crane was a weirdly shaped ladder. In fact, in places it *was* an actual ladder up the inside of the crane, only now and again we had to climb out and up the side of the structure. Still, it was as if we were climbing a ladder. I didn't know this then, but cranes are pretty much all the same. And from parkour you learn about materials – walls you come across, your trainers – and you build up a relationship with them. You learn what things you're going to get a good grip on, and what things you're not; you learn about foot placement and body weight and where to put it . . . It seems crazy, but today I could climb a crane angled at 45 degrees in the rain, get up there, look around, and be back down before the police arrive.

CRANES ARE PRETTY MUCH ALL THE SAME

But back on the Wirral, the night-time was almost unreal. It must have been a 75-metre crane, but you can't fully judge it in the dark. And it wasn't like being on a roof: there were just a few bars and railings, and that was it . . . air. But I had confidence in my own ability, and we reached the top without a hitch. I was comfortable sitting around up there. High up, it was a perfectly clear night on Merseyside. There was a full moon; we could see the building site and the lights of the housing estate below. In the other direction was the black mass of the Irish Sea.

There was a reasonable overhang on the back of the crane. I was sitting above Danny, and we were just chillin' on the weights on the back arm when, suddenly, he got down, eased himself over the edge and just hung off the crane. I thought: 'Ah, what? Fucking hell. *Shit!* This actually scares me.' Immediately I thought: 'I can't do that . . .' That really caught me off guard. Danny hung there for a couple of minutes. I don't think I could even balance on the top bar of the crane at that point.

HE GOT DOWN, EASED HIMSELF OVER THE EDGE AND JUST HUNG OFF THE CRANE

IT'S ABOUT YOU IN THAT MOMENT

Danny was amazing; he was super-chilled. I asked him what it was like. 'It's cool, man,' he replied, in his Scouse accent. He'd done it before. But we don't big things up; it's in our nature to underplay things, I suppose. Danny just clambered down there and did it. There was no, *'Wow! Check this out, man!'* It's not about what everybody else is doing, it's about you in that moment.

Later, back on the ground, back home in Southampton, I thought about it. Why couldn't I do that hang? Hanging is the easiest thing ever. Most people can hang from a bar for a minute or so. It's a basic move. You need to stay calm, and you need a bit of strength – but the only real challenge is in your brain. You have to dispel any negative thoughts or doubts. Normal people read more into hanging than there is. Jumping and flipping over rooftops is real high-level stuff; hanging is so simple . . . especially once you've done parkour. Later, the press and TV were always, 'Well, what does it *feel like*, hanging?' The answer is: it's a bit like hanging off anything else, really. I've never been one to hype things up.

Back then, before that climb up a crane on Merseyside, I'd hung off all kinds of rooftops. And it didn't take me long to understand why I might be scared of hanging from a crane – and also why I shouldn't be scared of it – because hanging really *is* easy. Hanging off something at 300 feet is the same as hanging off something at 3 feet…as long as you're in the right place, mentally. I think the darkness on Merseyside made it scarier as well.

I met Danny through parkour. Daniel is one of the best in the world, probably the most famous person in parkour – he's a legend, he's been doing it for well over a decade now. He's friggin' awesome, an amazingly capable dude. He's of Chilean ancestry, but has a sneaky grin that's pure Scouse. He used to have long hair like Jesus himself, and he's built like a tank, an absolute machine – a modern-day Hercules. I haven't seen him for a while now, but he's still like a brother to me. Danny is not only amazing at parkour but he just loves life – he's not all about going out and climbing shit – he's about living and doing fun things, exploring new experiences, which is what life should be all about. I'm the same.

HE'S ABOUT LIVING AND DOING THINGS

I COULD SEE THE LIGHTS OF LA TWINKLING HUNDREDS OF FEET BELOW

So, even though it had been Danny who took me up my first crane near Birkenhead, and he'd been the first person I'd seen dangle from the arm, we didn't go out to California in 2013 to jump stuff, in particular – it was more about hanging out with some of his friends out there, just living and seeing what came up. He knew some cool people on the West Coast, a few spots and places we could go. He introduced me to loads of people; we had a wicked time, in both LA and San Francisco.

One night we were bored, just driving around in our mate Will's old-school, classic American cop car – an LAPD vehicle from the seventies, one of those

where you change gear under the steering wheel, old sirens still intact. We cruised around, just watching the nightlife in downtown LA for a while. Then we saw this crane on a building site. We parked up and sneaked past some security guards who were chillin' out in a hut.

It was a pretty easy climb, up a ladder basically, but there was a security hatch right at the top. Every crane is different in terms of where the security hatch is. In the UK these tend to be quite low down, to stop yobs climbing up them. On this crane in LA you could climb practically to the top, all the way up to the security hatch just below the driver's cabin. Naturally, the hatch was locked, so we had to climb round the outside. But there were no beams or support or anything – just a gap from a kind of maintenance platform, which, if you could balance on a hydrant-shaped bollard on one leg, reach up with one arm, you could haul yourself up past the cabin and onto the arm. Because I'm 6 foot 3 inches tall I could just about reach up to that next level, hang on it with one hand and then pull myself up. If you fell off the bollard there was nothing to hold onto on the platform – you were gone. But it was all right; it wasn't too hairy. I could see the lights of LA twinkling hundreds of feet below, and we were almost surrounded by lit-up towers and buildings. It was calm; there was no wind. Once I'd grabbed onto the solid edge of the steel beam above, I knew I'd be all right: I couldn't ask for a better grip than that. You spend all your time looking for solid materials to lock onto then you know you'll be all right.

I STILL COULDN'T QUITE BRING MYSELF TO HANG OFF THE END OF THE CRANE

Danny is bang on 6 foot, so I had a few inches on him, and he couldn't reach the top beam. Once I was up there, I lay flat on the beam and he hung onto me and I just pulled him up. Then we walked out to the edge of the crane above the streets of LA. Coloured fairy lights were strung out along the arm of the crane as if around a cocktail bar. We could see flashing neon adverts and rooftops; this was different to Southampton. Dealing with air, and the gaps in girders, my spatial awareness and

foot-placement were fine. I was in good physical condition – physically, it was easy. I was beginning to overcome any mental weakness. It wasn't as scary as Birkenhead, but even though some people think that's me hanging there above the streets of LA on the film I released online, it's actually Danny. I still couldn't quite bring myself to hang off the end of the crane, but I felt like I was close to being able to do it. From up there the view was a bit *Blade Runner*, the illuminated tower blocks in the financial district of LA were pretty cool – you could see the Bank of America tower with its helipad on top. The crane was on the junction of South Hope Street and West 2nd Street, right above the wacky, twisted steel dome of the Disney concert hall.

We got down OK; we weren't caught, deported, tasered or shot.

That was my first long trip with Danny, and we did so much in California. We were in LA for most of the time and then we drove up the Pacific Coast highway to San Francisco for a few days. We swam off Malibu Beach, hung out in the Redwood Forests, camped beneath the biggest trees in the world, snuck onto a tourist submarine and a berthed warship whose pristine gold engine rooms were used in the filming of the *Titanic* movie. We messed around in shipyards, explored the Bay area; jumped off roofs into pools. Danny showed me how to live – and when I got back to the UK, I just wanted to live more: to go out, explore and see the world. I think I returned to England a far more capable individual.

You get music that means a lot to you, and you attach those tracks to film footage. You edit all those good moments to the songs you love, and a particular song comes to encapsulate those memories. For me, The Lumineers' 'Stubborn Love' will always be the soundtrack to that carefree, relaxed trip. We were young – and that's Danny – totally free.

DANNY SHOWED ME HOW TO LIVE

PARKOUR AND BURGER KING, THE HIGH STREET

SOUTHAMPTON

Parkour saved my life. It pulled me out of a depression; a low state… To say I'd had problems at school would be something of an understatement. In fact, a bit like pupils before me in Victorian England, I pretty much left school sometime around Year 10. Today, my motto is: Never look down. Don't look down in life, keep your head up and keep your chin up.

Growing up I was in a really bad position. I quit school, I had no GSCEs…nothing. To everyone else around me in Southampton I was on a downward spiral. Then I discovered something I loved, something I became passionate about. I trained, I developed; I got out of the hole I was in.

Weirdly, this all came about after I saw a commercial for BBC1. It featured a guy getting up from his desk, taking his shirt off, climbing out of his office window and then jumping across several rooftops, throwing himself perilously across ledges – all so he could beat the rush hour and get home in time to watch early-evening BBC1 TV. That was a really cool commercial. I remember thinking, 'What the heck is that?' It blew my teenage mind. Surely it wasn't real? It was first shown in 2002, but this would have been a couple of years after that – they used that short 'bumper' for ages. Around that time there was also a documentary on Channel 4 called *Jump London*, then a second one, *Jump Britain*. *Jump London*, opened with some

teenagers in joggers leaping over gaps between roofs to a beat-heavy soundtrack, while the presenter announced, in serious tones: '*This* is parkour, the anarchic new sport of free running…'

I was hooked.

It was a full-on documentary. Parkour originates from the French *parcours*, which is a kind of military training that involves overcoming obstacles in an emergency situation in the most efficient way. It was brought over to the UK, and to make it more commercial they changed the name to 'free running'. Instead of being about

efficiency it became more showy, more flippy, a kind of precursor to street dance. I remember watching that documentary and thinking, 'Man, this is amazing...'

At the time I was quite lost – I didn't really have anything I was passionate about. I loved playing computer games. That was it, though; that was all I would do back then. When we were young, myself and my cousin Dave – also a game nut – used to act out our own versions of *Metal Gear Solid* in his back garden. Then later, in our own back garden, inspired by this thing called parkour, myself and my stepbrother Wills started jumping over benches and hanging off trees, just silly childish stuff you do as kids.

Up until about Year 5 at school I'd been fine, but as I started to get older and understand things a bit more, I began to hate the system, to hate school. I hated being so controlled and forced to do things in certain ways. The idea of going to secondary school, an all-boys school, just scared the hell out of me. 'Why are we here? Surely this isn't what we are on this earth to do,' I used to think. At secondary school I particularly hated RE and English – when I was there, that is – being forced to read *Macbeth*. I didn't really over-think it, I just reckoned, 'Fuck it! What's the point? I can read and write.' And I got into a lot of trouble for not taking *Macbeth* home, for not turning up – but now I'm glad I did all that. I might have hated school, but I was

still smart – in top classes and everything – probably *too* smart. I understood it. I saw through school to the point where it wasn't right, you know? My attention span is too short anyway. I love films, stories in visual form. I've always been more of a visual kind of guy. But then one conflict, like with the English teacher over *Macbeth*, would lead to another – and it just got worse and worse and I got more and more tired of it, and so I was barely there.

Dave is my cousin, and later became my manager for a while, and he reckons around this time I was addicted to McDonald's Happy Meals and a right little hyperactive pain in the ass for my mum. The last bit of that might be the case, and it's true I have a bad habit of rocking in my chair and incessantly tapping my foot on the floor (in fact, my leg is pumping all the time while I'm simultaneously checking my phone, reading my emails, watching a video on YouTube, editing a film *and* writing this book). But I can focus completely and totally when the right thing absorbs me. That's how it has to be when you're several hundred feet up a crane.

Also, aged nine, I was diagnosed with coeliac disease, so Mum had to be really careful with my diet. I'd probably been coeliac all my life, but because of my intolerance to wheat and gluten, I suddenly had to start taking all my own food into school and living off baked potatoes as they didn't seem to have any alternative for me in the school kitchen. It was quite a tough school, just by a council estate in Millbrook, a suburb of Southampton, and I started to have trouble with a few of the teachers, one in particular who hated boys – so I used to really play up for her. Mum went in to see her and explained that I would co-operate and do the work if I was stimulated but if I were bored, I'd be a complete nightmare. The teacher just thought there was something wrong with me because

I rocked backwards and forwards on my chair a little too much for her liking. She really had it in for me.

It would be interesting to see what she made of me now.

My dad left when I was very young – I haven't seen him since I was eight – so for a while it was just my elder brother Danny, me and my mum, bless her, living for a while in a council flat on the edge of Millbrook. Being on the edge of the estate, on Lower Brownhill Road, we had a great view across fields and farmland. That was about a mile from where Mum grew up, and where my grandad still lived in his flat on the Mansel Park estate in Millbrook. Mum bought her flat and then sold it a few years later, after she'd met Pete, a GP, and we moved into a new place, literally round the corner in Hillyfields – a house that she and Pete renovated – then moved again, up the road to Nursling.

PARKOUR SAVED MY LIFE

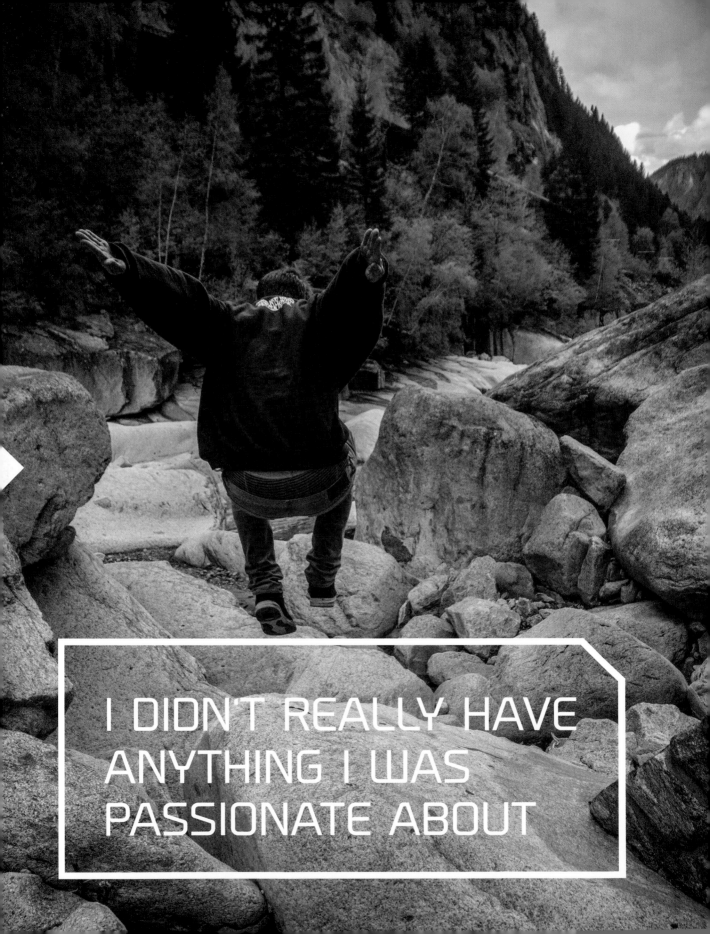

I DIDN'T REALLY HAVE ANYTHING I WAS PASSIONATE ABOUT

Mum and Pete were together for about ten years, in total, but it was around the time we moved to Nursling that I decided I didn't like school. Mum's a counsellor – she works with people who are struggling, but pretty soon her own life descended into pure chaos. She's supposed to be a person who knows how to help and how to do things right – she was working at four schools at the time, including mine, but that became difficult for her, what with her own son not turning up. Things turned out all right in the end, though. We got by, and it's not like we hate each other today, or anything – it was just a stressful moment in time. I remember Mum wrestling me to the floor on a couple of mornings, trying to get my clothes on. She was under pressure not only from the school but also from other adults, friends and relatives. There was this mantra we could never escape from: 'But *everybody* has to go to school.' We heard it so many times. Mum felt she was going mad. Her relationship with Pete ended, and this was a difficult time with my brother, Danny, who was ill.

I wouldn't go to school for ages, then the school would threaten: 'Well, we're going to take your mum to court.' So I'd go to school for two weeks, then leave again for another six months, and that seemed to work – at least until about the end of Year 10.

We moved out to Romsey, Hampshire, with Mum's new partner Ian, an electrician, and he got in on the pre-breakfast wrestling too, trying to bundle me into the back of the car. It might seem like our house was chaos, brawling at 8 o'clock in the morning and everything, but that wasn't the case at all for the rest of the day. Despite a few troubles, we settled down to being a calm, peaceful family. I got on well with my new younger stepbrother, Wills, and our home life became generally placid.

Which was a massive contrast with school. I remember one morning just staring into space during tutor, before lessons began, dimly aware of the teacher having an escalating row with a kid called Tino. He had a bit of a tough reputation, but he wasn't a bad kid – in fact, the older boys picked on him. Although whatever it was they were arguing about that day didn't go well for him: I was sitting on the front row, and he just turned round and smashed me in the face. He fractured my jaw, and it was years before the gap in my teeth closed up.

Another time, someone picked on a mate of mine who was deaf. This kid wasn't really a bully, just a bit of a dick: he'd try to be tough and bully the little guys, which is often how it goes. I wasn't interested in fighting at all, but he was in my face so I pushed him away. He slammed into a wall and crushed his new lunch box. 'You broke my fuckin' lunch box,' he whined before slapping me. I just punched him a few times, and then he was on the floor, crying. Afterwards I felt really bad – terrible – but he'd asked for it. That was the first time I ever punched anyone. I can't remember ever really throwing a punch again – if I did, I wouldn't have been able to fully commit to it. It's just not in me. However, after all this, combined with RE (it was a Catholic school), I pretty much decided, 'I'm done here.'

At one point Mum enrolled me in a local Montessori-like school that cost something in the region of £400 a month. It was a nice place and I did show up twice. Mum didn't pay for a second month, she got a home tutor in, which was OK, but I still had to read *Macbeth* and do things I didn't care for…

Apart from parkour, of course, which I really cared for, and to me seemed to represent total freedom. That turned everything around. Myself and my stepbrother Wills, Ian's son, started training properly around 2007. We were getting good at it. We'd improved over time; we'd learnt certain techniques, certain vaults. We started to run at, then climb an old brick wall at the back of our new house in Romsey. For ages we'd slip and fall, but we kept at it. I just had an inkling that parkour was some kind of release. Perhaps it was going to lead me to whatever it was that I was going to do in life.

I hadn't bothered turning up for my GCSEs. Then I literally did nothing but play computer games for a year, maybe two. When everybody else was doing A-levels I underwent a period of nothingness. I'd go to bed about seven in the morning, wake up around four or five in the afternoon, eat some food and then play computer games again all night. By then Mum was a bit worn down by it all. I didn't really have any friends, mainly because I didn't go to college, but this was the early days of the online gaming community and there was a nice sense of knowing people through that.

I'm still nocturnal now – which can be annoying, but only because it doesn't fit in with the professional world. I've never really had a proper job, a conventional job. The only way I got any money back in my *Call of Duty* days (or, rather, nights) was being a carer for my brother. Well, Danny had been ill, but he didn't really need help as such; he just needed someone to hang out with him. I was like, 'Yeah, of course. I'll get paid to just hang out with my brother!' He's the nicest guy, and those were some of our happiest days.

Danny moved out to Romsey, a small town just north-west of Southampton, with us, and when I wasn't with him I was attempting parkour with Wills – but we pretty soon began to grow out of leaping around the back garden. We looked on the internet and found a website – South Coast Parkour – which had forums for most of the cities on the south coast. Then one day, a bit like rookie skateboarders meeting up, we arranged to meet some of the more experienced parkour practitioners in Southampton. We used to meet up by the train station in Southampton. They were so much better than us, and a bit older, but we progressed.

Soon we became obsessed with it. Every day we were out for about ten hours at a time, just jumping around between walls – little walls at first – learning to roll properly on grass, perfecting certain vaults . . . really simple stuff. Then, gradually, over months, a couple of years, the jumps got bigger and higher. You build up the strength in your knees. (Remember: if you jump straight into it, your knees are going to explode; you'll do your back in, you're just going to wreck your joints.) Parkour is very gradual, very progressive – you build your body up slowly, otherwise you'll destroy it. It's fairly painstaking, but mentally you can evolve quite fast – your body just has to keep up. And because it's gradual you learn how to stay grounded and respect your body; you see things how they are and you problem-solve, so you really don't see things as dangerous. Today, I prepare myself so well and train so hard, I'm never really in a position where I think 'that's dangerous'. To me it's second nature – and that all comes from parkour.

When I was young I was a natural at picking things up super-quick: skating, BMXing, rollerblading, building ramps, and dropping in on them. I was that ballsy little kid who could drop in on a vert, never really afraid. My problem was I could never really stick at *most* things for long enough – most things, but not everything. I've got quite an addictive personality, so if I enjoy something I'll just go 100 per cent crazy at it. By the age of 18 or 19, I was done with the computer games: everything was fully parkour. That was it – every day, all day, repeating jumps hundreds of times. It just freed my head.

A typical day would involve meeting up with mates in town, right by the old Spar shop across from Southampton Central train station. It was also handy because I'd get the train in from Romsey. More often than not, I'd travel in alone (at first Wills was actually better than me at parkour – he was always stronger – but after a while he began to fade away from the scene). Outside Spar (I think it's a Co-op now) there was a lot of concrete: the concrete buildings, flats and shops, obviously, but also bollards and low walls. It was the perfect warm-up spot. There's some prickly bushes outside there today that probably exist thanks to us.

PARKOUR IS VERY GRADUAL, VERY PROGRESSIVE – YOU BUILD YOUR BODY UP SLOWLY, OTHERWISE YOU'LL DESTROY IT

We'd warm up, do joint rotations, all that boring stuff – stretching out, limbering up. There used to be pillars you could jump between outside the supermarket – that's all been knocked down and rebuilt now – and we used them to perform all kinds of little jumps as a part of our limbering-up routine. There were small jumps, nice low walls to do vaults over, a mixture of strides, running jumps and standing jumps – gaps everywhere, basically, that we could stride between or do running jumps across. Up by the station there'd always be a group of kids hanging around. It was the perfect starting spot. From there you'd build a rough schedule. There was another nice little spot by Asda and then we'd work our way down to the bottom of town, by the water. We were just long-haired kids messing about, like skaters without skateboards, but sometimes people told us to 'fuck off'. Most people didn't really pay much attention, though.

Well, that was until we started climbing up the side of the Halifax Building Society, and then they were like, '*Bloody hell!*' And when you start doing somersaults or jumping across gaps between ledges in a shopping precinct, people are like, '*Whoa, these aren't just kids!*'

The idea was never really, 'Let's climb up this building.' Getting higher was just a natural way of finding new challenges, of exploring – and of discovering new ways of dodging security guards. We started having these things called night missions. We'd meet at Spar again, but at midnight. I'd get the last train in from Romsey and be out all night (then get the first train home). We'd spend hours creeping around in the dark, sneaking up onto roofs on the High Street, because you couldn't really do that in the day time – people would be like, *'What the fuck are they doing on the roof of Primark?'* At night there was something a bit superhero(y) about it all; something very surreal…but also so real, because we'd trained so hard for it. But it was just like the stuff you see in films – creeping around, jumping over roofs, that was us. Just chillin', watching the sun come up over Southampton. During the night we'd find these massive roof gaps, but a lot of the time it was too dark to fully judge the depth or the distance, so we'd make a note to revisit them at a quiet time of day.

The basic techniques in parkour revolve around your vaults and your standing jump, or precision jump. A precision jump is a standing jump, with just a ledge to land on, so you have to be precise. If you've just got a railing to land on, you need to be extra-precise. You start between little kerbs, then move up through 'street furniture' – small pillars and bollards, then bigger bollards, or those electricity boxes with fences around them – then, after a while, you're mastering 8- or 10-foot-high walls across alleyways, or leaping from one edge of a building to another. You want to land on the opposite wall or ledge and 'stick it' without falling back, or overdoing it, your momentum carrying you over the other side. So you build up by finding a gap that's not quite your limit, and then you do it over and over again and work up to it until you can almost do it with your eyes closed, and then your level of skill moves up a notch and you move on again to a bigger jump. Then you repeat that one over and over again, until you work up to the human limit of jumping – for me, an average white male, that's about 11-and-a-half feet.

But then you move that gap up about 6 feet in the air and your brain senses a bit more danger. 'You can do this,' you tell yourself, because you've done it several hundred times before (albeit at a lower level, so you make the gap smaller, even more comfortable). Then you take it up another 10 feet – make the gap smaller again, and work up to it as before. Find a slightly bigger gap and before you know it you're 200 feet up in the air, jumping across a 10-foot gap on the roof of Burger King.

'YOU CAN DO THIS,'
YOU TELL YOUR-
SELF, BECAUSE
YOU'VE DONE IT
SEVERAL HUNDRED
TIMES BEFORE

In truth, at first I was quite scared of heights – in fact, I was *terrified* of them. But the whole idea of parkour is to push yourself and to get better so that you've conquered your fears and you're a more confident and stronger person all round. Now, of course, I couldn't care less when doing things that would scare the crap out of almost everyone else.

Parkour totally did represent a new beginning for me; it transformed me completely. I wasn't socially capable, I wasn't very good at life, but it turned things around completely. It gave me more confidence in every aspect of my life. Most people can appreciate that someone is good at running and jumping, somersaults and stuff, but they don't see the effect parkour has on you, generally – internally – as a person. The biggest thing about parkour is that it changes your outlook on everything, makes you a lot more grounded and level-headed – you can see things for what they are and deal with them in a good way. There's a bit more to it than getting really good at problem-solving, though: you become more aware of how you exist in the world, you start thinking about how you eat and sleep. You start looking at your surroundings, the city, in a different kind of way.

Southampton was heavily bombed during the Second World War, so there was a hell of a lot of rebuilding. There's a fair amount of what I guess would be termed 1960s 'urban space' – blocks of flats with courtyards and benches, shopping precincts and offices full of plazas, steps and rails; little bits of grass with some shrubbery. It's not simply because the author grew up here that Southampton forms the opening chapter of Owen Hatherley's book *A Guide to the New Ruins of Great Britain*. There's a shit load of weather-beaten, grey concrete everywhere – perfect for skating, jumping and running – and there's also been plenty of questionable redevelopment in the city of late. The cranes that dot the skyline don't all belong to the second largest container port in the country. My grandad's flat in Millbrook, near the Western Docks, was a low-level 1970s maisonette situated in a block above a row of shops – including the hardware shop he had the lease on. In his book, Owen Hatherley quotes the writer Jonathan Raban describing Millbrook as 'a vast, cheap storage unit for nearly 20,000 people'[1]. Today it probably does rank as one of the poorest places in the south, but we were happy there and we had a nice view of green fields.

---

1   Owen Hatherley, *A Guide to the New Ruins of Great Britain*, Verso Books, 2010.

The old Spar by the station stood in more or less the same complex as Wyndham Court, a famous piece of New Brutalist architecture, a block of flats and shops that looks like a gigantic concrete ocean liner. If Gateshead's Trinity Car Park hadn't been available for the filming of *Get Carter*, Wyndham Court might have sufficed. The pigeons and the rain have not been kind to the white concrete finish, but it's still an impressive structure. And inside there's a massive courtyard full of benches and ledges where we used to train before heading further into town. I think it's fair to say that growing up, my environment helped shape me.

In one of my very early films you can see me – mop-top, baggy tracksuit bottoms and all – shimmying up a drainpipe, past some round, ship-like windows at the back of an old brick building that housed telecoms equipment, internet servers and data storage (or something like that). It was what we knew as 'the Regent Street climb', part of our circuit that started on Regent Street, a little backstreet that nobody went down, apart from a few homeless people who slept there at night. That was a really cool place to climb – there were lots of little walls to jump between, multiple layers and levels, loads of fun stuff. The roof of the telecoms building was thick with aerials. You had to hang over a 10-foot drop, then crawl under some horrible barbed wire, before the climb culminated in a leap from the building that housed the old Phone Clinic shop across a gap to the block that still has Waterstones in there today, just by Barclays bank, near the Marlands shopping centre.

The same film sees me scaling a brick wall and climbing up the metal-grilled windows at the back of an old HSBC bank on the London Road. I shoot out from under a canopy, vault over a brick wall directly onto a narrow railing before flying across a pedestrian underpass onto the opposite narrow rail, then vault out into the road, Portland Terrace, just round the corner from Asda. All without breaking stride. Happy days!

Our favourite climb, though, was definitely the Burger King roof. The long, flat roof actually stretches from Burger King along the block, along the top of some offices above Poundland, Superdrug, Tesco Extra, Argos and a gym. It's up by the original Bargate, the crumbling gatehouse that is part of the old Norman town wall that fortified the city. (I've been up there too; and also on the roof of the old Bargate shopping centre.)

FOR AGES WE'D SLIP AND FALL, BUT WE KEPT AT IT

The Burger King roof is known as 'the Burger King roof' because that was where we'd get in. We'd climb over the brick wall at the back of Burger King, where they keep all the bins, go up some stairs, balance along a couple of walls, up a ladder onto the roof, and then edge around this rusty white overhanging fence, which for some reason separates the roofs of Superdrug and Tesco. We'd then head up another ladder, pop up over a wall, past some air-con units, and there, standing before you, were these two random buildings – electrical or air-con units (one of them made a loud drone or whooshing noise all day), or some kind of entrance housing a staircase and a chimney. Today they're still there, sitting on top of the roof of the gym above Tesco and Argos. The buildings are pretty high, separated by a gap of about 10 feet, effectively six or seven stories up – get that wrong and there's just a sheer drop to the backstreet below.

That gap was one of the first high ones I jumped. Now I can somersault over it, but back then that was *the one*, a leap across those two random blocks on the roof of Burger King – real high-up, scary stuff. That was a great roof, a formative roof: you had to just read it, and get really good at reading the layout. I could do somersaults and jumps at a fairly low level very comfortably, but that roof really helped me push myself, to overcome my fear of heights.

Another one of those early films finishes with me doing a backwards somersault on the ledge of the roof above Burger King. It's daybreak, but the lights are still on in the shop windows of the deserted High Street below. By that point, around 2009, we'd totally surpassed the older parkour dudes. Their mentality was quite limited. They were really good the first six months or so, but then we shot past them. That's how it works with skaters today – same with parkour guys – the 12-year-olds will be doing things that took somebody 12 years to learn; 12-year-olds can do now what professional skateboarder Tony Hawk took years to perfect. I was part of the new generation of parkour that learned things really fast. The older generation passed on everything on to us and we surpassed them. Now there are 10-year-olds doing crazy things on roofs because we've passed everything *we* know on to *them*. Unfortunately for other mums out there, there are 10-year-olds doing that jump on the roof of Burger King today.

When our parkour mates started coming up to Romsey on their bikes to do stuff in the garden it felt like we could all breathe again. My stepbrother Wills is a really nice personable dude, people are comfortable around him; he had friends. I can't really credit him enough for the effect he had on me: he was a major influence in my life, in bringing me out of myself. Mum was happy too. Parkour felt like an absolute godsend to her as well – her son was starting to act normal; he wanted a trampoline in the back garden. Wills and I saved up and installed what became the first item in our new training area.

But it wasn't long before Mum got wind of what was really going on when I caught the train into Southampton to see my new friends. She was worried about me hanging around, getting into trouble with other kids down there. Then she was really shocked when she saw an early film of me balancing and walking along a wall by Primark – then suddenly doing a backward somersault on it. *'Jesus Christ,'* she yelled, *'he's going to break his neck!'* She caught sight of the video while round at one of my new mates' houses.

'Oh bless him, isn't he clever?' said my mate Rich's mum.

'Yeah, you might not think that if was *your* son,' was Mum's reply.

• • •

In 2009, I went on another trip that changed my life.

In the loitering-around care-allowance days, Danny and I used to fly remote-controlled aeroplanes and stuff. We inherited that from our grandad, who was friggin' awesome. Despite living in a council flat in Millbrook he had all the gadgets, the first computers and stuff; and he even owned an actual aeroplane, which he kept at Thruxton Aerodrome. He'd learnt to fly (in a glider) aged 40 – despite being dyslexic, he got through a series of tough written exams – and, aged 55, he did a skydive with Mum. He was eccentric, but he was awesome. He got us into remote-control planes, and we still love them to this day: remote-control cars, drones…all that stuff. Grandad was in the Navy – he just loved adventure, and had so many amazing stories it would blow our minds. A bit of a risk-taker too, he used to say he turned his mum's hair prematurely grey.

I remember shortly after he died – at the time when I was getting really serious about parkour – a bunch of friends, five of us, were planning a trip to Sardinia. The idea was to stay in a forest, catch and eat fish, sleep in hammocks…just sort of disappear and live off the land, retreat to wilderness, go back to nature, leave the system behind us and spend a lot of time swimming and being free. I said to Mum, 'I really want to do this, but I'm a bit worried I don't have much money.' She just said, 'James, what would Grandad say? He'd say, "Just do it. Just book it and go."' And that was the first time I really thought, 'Yeah, fuck it, just do it. Just jump straight in.' It's literally how I live now: pure spur of-the-moment stuff.

So we flew into Cagliari and then took a long bus-ride to the forest. That was the beginning of my life of random adventures, learning about the world and how everything works. We did loads of training out in the Sardinian wilderness, jumping between walls, walking for miles into the forest, sleeping on the pebble beach on the south of the island, stringing up hammocks near the beach. We'd sleep on the beach then wake up to the sound of the waves, 'Whoosh…' There were massive rocks to dive off into the sea; the water was perfectly clear. It was a dream – we were living on a natural parkour course.

As I've said, the whole thing about parkour is that it isn't just the physical stuff: it changes your outlook on everything.

Parkour and that holiday made me want to live. I didn't have to be jumping around and climbing, I just wanted to get out there and see things and experience new things. That was what parkour became more about, rather than just jumping around. Now, when I get back into this country from a foreign trip, and you see those customs and border guards – the ones who are out to get you – I tend to think, 'I just don't like it that much here.' I've been all over the place now, but the most depressed country I've been in is the UK. I really like England, but if you hang around too much with depressed people, you just get depressed yourself. Looking at people who are pissed off and sad isn't enjoyable. The happiest place I've been to? India, and there are people there with absolutely nothing. They're the happiest people and the nicest people – it's a crazy world, isn't it?

Back in Southampton from Sardinia I realised there was so much more out there, so many people. Most people in this world they wake up, they go to work, they finish work, they have dinner, they watch TV, they go to bed – on repeat. That's life for a lot of people. Fair enough, some people enjoy it, but you can see that some don't. Most people, you see it in their eyes: they're stressed out, pissed off at life, they're not happy in the slightest.

Nowadays, if I go out into town and jump around everyone looks at me. The attention is massive. Every time I go out in Southampton, I get recognised. People say: 'Hey, James, I love your work,' or ask for photos. Or if I'm climbing: 'It's that guy on the roof of Primark again!' But I don't need to do that so much now because I've trained for so long; the only thing that deteriorates is my stamina. These days, I'm not so addicted that I feel the need to go out training every day for hours on end. I could wake up tomorrow and have no interest in climbing again, and that'd be fine. There are other things I want to do. The interest in parkour has faded quite a lot. I still love to move and do stuff, but I do it when I feel like it. I love creating stuff now – film, mainly – I'm happy with that. I'll still go out at night on my own when it's dead, and there's no unwanted attention.

There are no cameras on the rooftop of Burger King. That really is an amazing rooftop: everything you could need to train is there – walls to hang onto and climb, jumps to do, rails to balance on; it's a whole world. If I'm feeling slow or lazy or sluggish, I'll go out on my own, go up there for a few hours and just go nuts.

I REALISED THERE WAS SO MUCH MORE OUT THERE

3

SOUTHAMPTON CRANE

THE START OF THE GOLDEN HOUR IS 4:15 TO 4:30 IN THE MORNING

Today, looking out of the window of my flat in Southampton's redeveloped waterfront, there's a massive glass tower, the Moresby Tower. The crane that built this block of luxury apartments must have been 100 metres high: a massive 330-foot tower crane that went straight up.

In May 2013 I was back home from Merseyside, riding around on my motorbike, seeing what had changed while I'd been up north. I rode down to the waterfront and spotted these three massive cranes. Trouble was, I was about to head off again – this time to California, just for a few weeks' holiday with Danny and his mates out there (see Chapter One). I saw the cranes, one particularly tall one, and thought, 'Fuck! I really want to climb that.' But I didn't have time. My mate Gibbs had seen the cranes as well. In fact, he'd texted me before I went away. We'd had the same vision.

Anyhow, I went to America with Danny, thought about things, and maybe returned a different person, more free, more confident. I came back and was straight out on the bike, driving around again: yes, they were still there! I phoned up Gibbs: 'Let's do it.' And the following Sunday, at 4 a.m., we met in the car park beneath the tallest of the cranes. Well, we were supposed to meet in the car park, but Gibbs and Doug weren't there when I parked up the bike. They hadn't bothered waiting for me; already they were partway up the crane, sitting on a beam by this padlocked security hatch.

Doug – a smart bugger who was doing a Masters in physics at the time – was trying to crack the possible combinations of the code…starting at zero. I got there, and I was like, 'What are you doing?' Parkour people, we are addicted to challenges and problem-solving. But I said, 'Dude, that's a complete waste of time.' The sun wasn't quite up, but it was going to be a beautiful morning – and we didn't have all day. At the side of the hatch were these anti-climb metal sheets, bolted down to cover a gap. Nowadays this kind of thing is even worse (thanks to me) – so I just sort of pushed them in. The metal was only a couple of millimetres thick – they were flaps, really –

painted red. I bent them in and squeezed through the gap between the hatch and the side of the crane. It was a tight squeeze, but it meant we didn't have to bother with the code.

The start of the golden hour is 4:15 to 4:30 in the morning. As we climbed up the crane the view was just beautiful, absolutely ridiculous – the whole of the city, the docks, the river Itchen, the Solent, all glowed. Again, the climb was easy – a ladder, basically. All the way up the sun was breaking across the horizon. At the top we calmly walked out along the metal rail, about a foot wide, towards the flashing red aeroplane light at the end of the crane. Below was the marina, little white boats parked in neat lines.

I sat on the white metal frame of the crane and manoeuvred myself down, just as I'd seen Danny do on Merseyside and in LA. My grip was strong. This was the first time I actually hung off a crane – over the harbour, at 4:30 in the morning. It was just beautiful. People always ask me what I was thinking about at that moment but there was nothing, really. I was calm. There was a sense of complete bliss. I was chilled, thinking about what I might eat for breakfast, 'cos I was starving.

I can hang for a couple of minutes. Because I was filming I did it three times: once without the camera, just me and the crane and no other thoughts at all – you can't afford to think negative things. If you think negative things then the chances of something negative happening are probably quite high, right? If you worry

about slipping all the time, there's way more chance you'll actually slip. You've got to commit: it's all or nothing. The second time I hung with the camera in my mouth, which gives you the best, most solid shot.

As soon as you've hung once, you think, 'Ah, why was I scared of that? I'm not

even scared of this.' Once you've done
it one time you can do it anywhere again
– it's like that with most things in parkour.
The challenge is always the first time, and
it's always the mental thing: 'Shit, that
looks really hard.' Then you do it – 'Oh, it's
not, it's super-easy.' Then you've just got it.
It's done; you move on.

The third hang I did the same thing, but with Gibbs perched above, filming me. Doug was really scared and sat a few feet away on a girder, held back by his own fear. He's bloody clever, super-smart, geeky and he knows everything . . . but he's very scared of things, too. It didn't affect me, though. We all do the same thing, but we're all different – and that's really cool.

It was dead quiet – the perfect sunrise, no real wind. Just spot on. I decided I was going to walk across the top beam, which was 6 inches wide. As soon as I stood up . . . and this is the last thing you hear on the film . . . there was a police siren. Someone had phoned the police. If you watch the film, and study the footage of the ground from the crane, you can see my bike in the car park, and just behind that there's a wall. Behind the wall there's a police van, just creeping along. They were probably shitting themselves, and I guess the moment I stood up, they thought, 'Fuck this,' and turned the siren on.

It was time to leave. We climbed down. They were waiting for us at the bottom. I hid the cameras because I knew the footage would be good. But they didn't actually care – they were so blown away by the fact I had actually stood on the top beam. Back then this was all quite new to everyone. As usual, there was a good cop and a bad cop – one was a grumpy bastard, the other one quite nice. But if someone's going to be a knob, I haven't got time for it.

WE ALL DO THE SAME THING, BUT WE'RE ALL DIFFERENT – AND THAT'S REALLY COOL

The grumpy guy started, and I couldn't even be bothered to listen – he'd clearly got out of the wrong side of bed – but the other guy, he was really cool. He was like, 'What the fuck are you doing? You just stood on top of that crane.' I was like, 'Yeah, it's fairly normal for us.' He just shook his head and said, *'Fuckin' hell!'* He couldn't believe it – in Southampton of all places. Nothing happens here, especially at 6 o'clock on a Sunday morning. They took our details, the usual stuff, and sent us off with a 'Don't do that again' warning.

That was it – great fun. The rest of the day was a bit of an anti-climax.

Afterwards, somebody sent us some pictures. They'd been watching from the ground, and you can see the three of us up on the crane, silhouetted against the clear blue sky. They're like freeze-frames from a crime scene: Doug sitting down (looking tense); me and Gibbs hanging off; me about to stand up on the top beam; the three of us trooping back down the ladder to the police.

I CAN HANG FOR A COUPLE OF MINUTES

I know what to do these days to not
get caught. It's simple stuff, really. We
were up there way too long – over two
hours. We got lost in the moment, a bit
carried away because it was so good. I
put it down to beginners' inexperience.
Someone woke up, looked up from their
balcony, saw us and phoned the police.
Now I realise you either do things in the
middle of the night – and stay up the
crane as long as you want – or, if you
need to film it, get up there at 4 or 4:30 in
the morning and be up and down within
an hour and, usually, you're all right. That
depends on where you are, of course.
Looking out of my window today, I could
go and climb up the red crane I can see
in the distance, completely ignore anyone
who saw me, and I'd probably be able to
sit up there for half an hour or so before
the police arrived. Once I'd climbed
down, they'd be like, 'Oh, you again,' and
maybe take my details.

I've never been to court; there's no
real reason for an owner of property to
waste time suing me. There's no criminal
damage. I haven't stolen anything – it'd
be a waste of time. And now I've got an
online presence it's even easier to prove
what I do. Round here the police know
me, anyway. Most of the time they're like,
'Well, if we'd known for sure it was you
we wouldn't have bothered coming out.'

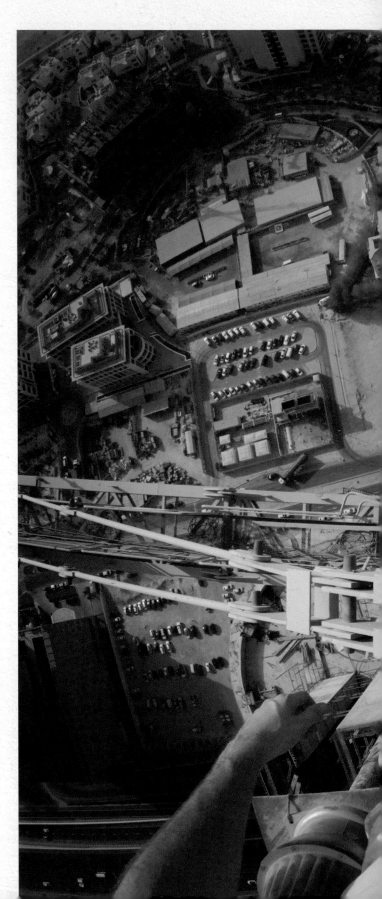

WE GOT LOST IN
THE MOMENT

UKRAINE

THEY TAKE THINGS TO THE NEXT LEVEL

Everything blew up after I released the video of that first climb in Ocean Village. It went viral; it seemed the whole world wanted to look at the view hanging from a crane above Southampton marina.

I put it up online about a month after we'd shot it. At the time, June 2013, I had a job in Brighton, which essentially involved being a model for new Triumph motorcycles, riding around on new Triumph Bonnevilles all day. I released the film one evening, then rode down to Brighton the next morning, arrived at the hotel, got ready to do the job, checked my YouTube page and realised I had 200,000 hits! 'What the fuck is going on?' was all I could think. Then, throughout the day, my phone didn't stop ringing; my emails were going crazy. Over the next few days I was on all the radio stations, TV too: BBC1, ITV – everything. Within a week the film had had a million views and went up to 2 million the following week. It was being watched all over the world, social media was going crazy, and *Good Morning USA* had got in touch.

A few days later, I got a phone call from Firecracker Films, a production company who do stuff for Channel 4. They'd recently pitched a show to them about Russian free climbing – the Russians are famous for this kind of thing, because they're mental, basically – and Channel 4 loved it, but they wanted someone English to front the programme. Firecracker's meeting with Channel 4 took place the day after I'd released my video, so everything just synced-up perfectly. A week after that I was standing underneath a crane by the waterfront in Southampton being interviewed by a cameraman for a dummy pilot. Channel 4 came back a day later and said, 'It's a no-brainer – let's go, let's do it.' Before I knew it contracts were signed and a TV crew was at my house, making a documentary on my life.

A key part of the programme was to be a trip to Kiev to meet Ukrainian free climber Mustang Wanted. We filmed some stuff in Southampton that summer – my failed attempt to climb the red crane by the waterfront (see the next chapter) – and set off for Ukraine in October.

Without wishing to generalise the Russian –Ukrainian thing too much: they're all nuts. They take things to the next level, that's what they're known for. Their stunts look like they could be staged in the *Don't Look Down* TV documentary, but Mustang telling me about the guy who back-flipped 16 stories to his death in St Petersburg, and

his friend who got electrocuted climbing up a radio mast ('We didn't check if it was switched on') was genuinely the first thing he told me. We'd just met, in a park near where Mustang lived, and he was recounting the tale of some guy who'd been electrocuted, and all the time he was kind of smirking at me – you know: 'You could die too.'

Before that, the first contact we'd had was when he emailed me in advance, asking how much I weighed. I could see his line of thinking, but I replied, 'I'll hang you, never the other way.' Happily, I was too heavy for him anyway: 'Ah, that's a shame, James. I can't hold that much.' Mustang is tiny – I wouldn't put my life in his hands. Looking at some of his films online, he seems to get a kick out of his life being out of his hands – there's some footage of him walking out on a plank from the top of a tower block; only a couple of his friends are sitting on the other end of the plank – whereas I'm the opposite, it all has to be under my control. I know what I can do. I don't like things that are out of my control – I guess I'm a bit of a control freak. (I don't like rock-climbing or bouldering and I don't trust cliff faces – who knows what could be working its way loose? I hate the idea of base jumping, or any kind of jumping out of an aeroplane with a parachute where your life is in your back pack. If you pull that cord and it doesn't go, and you pull the other cord and it doesn't go . . . that's it.)

October in Kiev is not unlike January in Britain – it was cold. One of our first trips in the capital was to the Dnipro Towers, five half-built residential skyscrapers near the district of Troieschyna that have been abandoned because of the financial situation in Kiev – the money just ran out, so the uninhabited husks, empty shells, sit in a bleak and muddy fenced-off building site. I was obviously super-excited – they looked amazing. They were fenced all the way round; two security guards with dogs were patrolling the perimeter in a circuit. We had to sit outside the gap in the fence and watch for them going past – as soon as they'd passed out of earshot we slipped through the fence, legged it and ran straight into the building, then climbed up a lift strut to get to the bottom of the stairs. There were loads of stairs all the way up.

I WOULDN'T PUT MY LIFE IN HIS HANDS

We got to the top; it was a chilly morning – freezing, in fact – but it was so cool up there. I had that Christmas-morning feeling. There was a fantastic climbing frame, a bit like a giant-sized washing-line carousel, the outer rings of which extended out over the edge of the tower, 35 stories, 110 metres in the air – just my kind of thing. I was loving it – it's rare that you get something that high with just about everything you could want: railings all over the place and jumps, it was awesome, one of the best places I've been. And a structure on top of a structure was the icing on the cake.

Mustang had been up there many times before, of course – so when he jumped out onto the narrow white bars of the radial construction, if it was as if he were walking down the street whistling, going to get a loaf of bread. All the while he was quite calm, pretty chilled, listening to classical music on his headphones. He listens to music all the time, and not just classical. During the trip his headphones were permanently clamped on under his beanie hat. People think we're crazy adrenaline junkies who just go nuts to heavy metal or

something, but we're not like that at all. On the roof of the tower we were so far above everyone else – the city – we had no worries of being seen at that height. The view was immense: loads of run-down housing estates and apartment blocks. Mustang lived in one of those flats, with his mum. I stayed there on a second trip back to the city – it was a rough block, but their apartment had a nice, homely feel to it, and his mum was really sweet. She is similar to mine like that: every night she made a cute little dinner, a Ukrainian dish of potatoes and meat. You could see that she was worried about Mustang, but she was always smiling and happy. She sent me back to England with a small Ukrainian teapot, like a little milk urn, for my mum.

I think everything is relative to where you come from: you can't remove your behaviour from the context of where you grow up. And in Kiev there are limited opportunities.

I HATED HOW HE COULD PUT SO MUCH TRUST IN THINGS HE COULDN'T CONTROL

For Mustang, the whole Channel 4 programme was a sort of rerun of his greatest hits, all the spots that he'd done, and been hanging from for years – so there wasn't anything particularly new or challenging for him. He just loved the fact the camera crew was there, and that he'd been paid for the use of some archive footage. There's not much for him in Kiev: there's no money there, no wealthy TV production companies, no Ukrainian version of Channel 4 – or, at least financially, not on the same scale. To be famous on a global stage would be very beneficial for him, but he's trapped in Kiev.

If you watch the footage of Mustang walking around the frame on top of the Dnipro Towers, he seems less sure-footed than me, and he says himself that he can often slip, or be caught out by a gust of wind. It's because, basically, he's a climber. I'm perhaps a bit more fluid, better at movement as a whole than him, because Mustang doesn't have any parkour training. His skills are more specific – if he's not walking or hanging onto something, then he's a bit out of his zone – and perhaps that also explains why he has to put a lot of trust in other things. Maybe that's all he's got. He's practised climbing and balancing, but not parkour and free running. He's not very agile, but he's incredibly strong. He can do five straight one-arm chin-ups on each arm, which is indicative of super-human strength. He's got the perfect build – powerful on top, but with tiny little legs. He's got decent balance, but that's all – he can't really jump.

No one really knows a great deal about Mustang, like where he's from. He was on the run from the military for about two years, having bunked his National Service – hence the name 'Wanted'. That's where he created his persona. His reasons for urban free climbing are completely different to mine: we come from totally different cultures. Life is so different there to what we're used to in Britain. There's no money, no work, there's literally nothing to do; the old Soviet council housing is pretty grim. Mustang has been climbing tower blocks and doing dangerous things since he was 16. Walking to the end of a 450-metre crane in the snow dressed only in his underpants and a silver crash helmet is normal for him. Perhaps life has a different value over there, or maybe somehow it isn't quite so valuable to them. Lives are harder, perhaps they just don't care so much, or don't have as much to live for – and death is a bit more pervasive in parts of eastern Europe than here in the far west of the continent, where such a fuss is made over it.

There was something in Mustang's eyes when he was talking so matter-of-factly about his friend who had been electrocuted – it didn't seem to faze him. It's a bit like in the TV series *The Wire*, when the black kids wrapped up in the drugs world in Baltimore just shrug when they learn someone has been 'deaded'. In Russia and Ukraine, in every area of life, things get pushed that little bit further, and so the people take more risks, as death seems to be more normalised. At one point on a rooftop, Alex, the director, asked Mustang: 'Aren't you worried you're going to die?' Mustang laughed, and replied: 'Alex, haven't you heard? I have bad news for you: we are all going to die.'

While we were on the roof of the Dnipro Towers, I caught the first sight of the Moscow Bridge. I knew we were going to do that. It was clear Mustang was pretty keen on 'the hang' – me dangling him off the edge of the bridge, one-handed – even though he'd done that before too, with some of his mates. I'd seen it in some of the footage he'd released online, filmed in winter-time: Mustang in just boxer shorts again.

We went there a day before we actually climbed it, just to look at it – it was so cool, such a weird and unique-looking cable-bridge across the Dnieper river. It stands 120 metres high from the road (which is practically a motorway) – about 180 metres from the water. Steel cables sweep from the road bridge up to the top. They were a bit of a nightmare to climb, to be honest – they're taut and start a good foot or more wide, but then they taper towards the top, so you've got these massive fat cables right next to each other which you can't put your feet in between. They also sway in the wind. Still, the next afternoon it was fine following Mustang up them. Even with the cables wobbling and whistling in the breeze off the river, and the din from the rush-hour traffic below making it almost impossible to speak, I didn't have to worry about him. The climb to the top was relatively brisk and straightforward. Once there I found myself looking back at the Dnipro Towers.

I wasn't that worried about hanging him off either – I knew I could hold him (we'd had a couple of dry runs on a tower block, a few days before) and I knew there was a secure railing up there that I'd be able to hook myself over. There was no risk for me – nor for him – unless he tried to let go.

He didn't. In no time, he shifted himself off the edge, gripped my hand, then with a 'Yah, man!' was swinging from my hand, happy to have me suspending him above the traffic and the icy blue of the Dnieper below.

The idea of doing a back-flip on top of the bridge had been fermenting in my head before we climbed the cables, but there was no way of knowing what I'd be dealing with in terms of space until I got to the top. But as soon as I got up there, I was like, 'Yeah, I'm going to back-flip on this.' In the film, as I'm psyching myself up, Mustang eggs me on, hurries me up – *'James, James . . . the, er, police people are here!'* I think the police had been down there for about 20 minutes while I was preparing to do the flip. I'm not quite sure what they were doing – waiting for us to come down, I guess. I was super-nervous, but the flip was good – I have, after all, done a thousand back-flips on the roof of Burger King in Southampton. Mustang was super-excited when I did the back-flip on the bridge. He doesn't do any kind of acrobatics, so that blew his mind – *'Faack! James! Yaas, man!'* I was still nervous, but for me it was super-easy, really. I did another (better) flip so I was completely satisfied. . .

Mustang started climbing down the front of the huge bronze fascia at the top of the bridge's column. He was holding onto it with just his fingers stuck into the grooves of the metal shield, and you could see it coming away from the concrete when he put his weight on it. As he clambered to the bottom, his fingers wedged into the relief of the design, he realised that his shoelace was undone, so he tied it up while perched on a narrow ledge. That was just horrible! Alex, filming on the ground, had his head in his hands. The bridge had been built in 1976 – God knows how firmly that metal shield was mounted, what level of corrosion might have taken place over four decades. I hated how he could put so much trust in things he couldn't control – he didn't seem to have a care in the world.

Once he'd finished up by the shield, Mustang shot back down to the ground. I wasn't too slow going back down the wobbly cables behind him although it could appear as though my leisurely descent was the reason behind us being arrested on the bridge. But I never worry about the police anyway – they're just a distraction you don't want . . .

. . . Especially after three hours in a police station. We'd been picked up by the much-feared Ukrainian special police but we knew we hadn't really done anything wrong. Mustang suggested maybe they could just let us go, save us all a bit of time, but the head of security on the bridge started panicking about the possibility of us having left explosives up there, so we ended up being driven to a local station. Quite why an Englishman would want to blow up a bronze shield, presumably a symbol of Ukrainian power, pride, strength and independence, off the top of a bridge wasn't raised, and once at the station, the police didn't seem that clear about what they were doing, or what was going on. Mustang was still relaxed: 'Well, yeah, fine, whatever.' They know him like they know me in Southampton.

We were there for what seemed like an eternity. The police didn't appear to want to be there either; they seemed bored, filling out endless forms, which we then had to sign. The translator told me, 'Every time Mustang goes in, they say, "You again?!"' They let us go – it was no big deal, really.

I went back to Kiev a week or so after filming had finished because I'd enjoyed myself so much, and because I'd met a girl, a hotel receptionist. The second trip, I stayed with Mustang and we shot a lot more stuff, climbed a few more bridges – nothing as big as the Moscow Bridge – hung off a couple of other tall buildings,

and rode the trains. On the underground in Kiev you can jump between the trains and ride the platforms connecting them. That's probably the silliest thing I've done – trying to balance on the connecting platform between two carriages on a speeding train through a tunnel at 80mph. In the UK, there are covers between carriages to prevent that kind of behaviour, but out there they don't give a crap, and you can basically do what you want on the trains.

We went to loads more old apartment blocks, run-down towers and bridges, but that was the last time I saw Mustang. Kiev was cool at the time, and I got some good insights into life there, but me and Mustang, we're on completely different wavelengths. I was happy to do it for him, to hang him from the bridge, that first time – I knew I had no bad intentions – but I would *never* hang off his arm (or anyone else's). One time we were filming on the edge of a roof, and he pulled me back towards the edge – this was at a massive height, a narrow ledge on what must have been a 20- or 30-storey building – then he tried to shove me, like those people who, when you're leaning back on your chair, will suddenly creep up behind you and pull you backwards to try to scare you. I was quite surprised he did that. '*Yes, James shat his pants*' – but I have no interest in doing that to other people. There was another time he tried to rough me up a little bit, have a bit of a grapple, but that's not my thing. I never really get angry – I was twice his size anyhow.

Mustang loves fighting. They have organised fights in Ukraine. There are online forums, where people arrange to meet in a park, or wherever, and a huge brawl – a massive ruckus between 100 or so Ukrainian heavies – ensues. And sometimes people die in these fights.

I wasn't so keen on all that. That's a very different kind of adrenaline rush; a thrill-seeking experience I'm happy not to seek out. Outside of climbing, Mustang's on edge. He's a different guy to the one listening to classical music on a rooftop.

In fact, everybody seemed on edge most of the time I was in Ukraine. Not long after I left for the second time in 2014, everything kicked off in Kiev. The main square we'd been hanging out in, filming – Independence Square, or Maidan Nezalezhnosti – turned into a riot zone during the uprising; people were tearing down Soviet statues, ready to rip everything to shreds. Once the war was fully underway, Mustang climbed the Kotelnicheskaya building in Moscow, one of the Seven Stars, the famous Stalinist skyscrapers. He painted the spire blue and yellow and draped the Ukrainian flag from the top of the building. It was all over the news and he became something of a hero in Ukraine. Incredibly, some Russian base jumpers who'd climbed the building with him that day took the flack. Mustang somehow got away with it and, despite later coming forward, claiming he'd acted alone and offering to hand himself over to the Russian authorities in exchange for the

detained, the others are still in jail. That's Russia – a mad place.

I felt like I'd made some kind of connection with Mustang when we parted, but since the problems with Russia have kicked off, he's gone a bit off-piste. Once the *Don't Look Down* TV show went out and I started to blow up, I sensed Mustang changed his tone – a bit of rivalry crept into things. He's quite competitive; he always wants to be the best, whereas I hate all that; I've no interest in competing. But I can see his point – it's not his fault Channel

4 wanted an English guy rather than a Ukrainian free climber. Things cooled when I started making money from my online profile too. But, again, I can see where he's coming from, because they've got nothing in Ukraine. He hasn't released anything for a while. I'm sure he still has his fanboys out there, but the films of smuggling hot girls up onto rooftops to take cool pictures of them – balancing on girders, having a party, eating cheesecake on a crane – seem to have dried up. Maybe the Ukrainian teenagers are moving on to bigger, better things.

I'd definitely go back there again. The special police may be crazy, but there are loads of great climbs. It's a really interesting place. I love grotty run-down urban environments – they're ideal for me to do my stuff in; the climbing and exploring – and some of the most beautiful women in the world seem to live in Kiev.

But to live there permanently? Maybe that wouldn't be so cool.

MUM WORRIES, DISUSED GAS-HOLDER, THE WEATHER, AMBIENT MUSIC

SOUTHAMPTON

I WANTED A SOUND-TRACK THAT WAS CALMING AND UPLIFTING

On the Channel 4 documentary *Don't Look Down* there's a scene filmed in Mum's kitchen in Romsey, just me and her. She's worrying about my climbing, as I'm sitting on the worktop, eating some raw parsnips she's preparing. It's not quite clear who she's cooking for; the impression is there's just the two of us living in a big empty house. But the reality was there were six of us living there then: myself, Mum and Danny, and Ian and his kids – Wills and Alex (Ian's other daughter, Vix, was away at the Brit School in London). We were a normal family – well, apart from the climbing cranes business.

That empty house was an unavoidable part of the filming process; what the TV programme captured really accurately was Mum's sense of rising anxiety. She'd seen my friend Danny hanging from the crane in LA on Facebook while we were still out in America. At first she panicked and thought it was me but I reassured her it was Danny.

YOU CAN'T AFFORD TO HAVE A MISHAP BECAUSE YOU'RE TOO EXCITED

'Just because he's doing that and he's your mate, you don't have to follow him, because that's like, a really crazy thing to do,' she pointed out over the phone.

'Yeah, Mum,' I laughed.

But a chill went down her spine – she could see the extent to which some people were prepared to go to.

Then my brother Danny said to her one day, 'He's been up climbing cranes.'

'No, he hasn't, he's got more sense than that,' Mum replied.

I said, 'Well, er, yeah. Actually . . .' and I had to show her the Ocean Village crane hang by the marina in Southampton. This was before I'd released it – it was still raw, I hadn't finished editing it. She found it quite difficult to watch but she said that it was a lot easier because I was sitting there next to her.

In those early days Mum constantly had to weigh up me being happier than at any time since I'd 'left' school with what it was that was actually making me happy. She'd have loved to be able to climb the cranes herself – she loves rock climbing, so she's got a sense of the wonder and awe of being at a great height, but the hanging thing was a stretch too far.

Once I'd released the film, she also had to put up with some people saying, 'This is fantastic – what he does is incredible.' But on the other hand, there were plenty of dissenting voices, accusing her of being irresponsible for letting me do it. She often had to point out that I was technically an adult, over the age of consent.

Around this time she took a train journey to a working therapy weekend with her ex-partner Pete, who Danny and I and Mum had lived with for a time in the Hillyfields area of Southampton (just round the corner from Millbrook), then a bit further up the road in Nursling. Pete is also a trained therapist, and he'd clocked my new-found fame and notoriety. He was pretty unequivocal: 'You have to tell him to stop it.' A couple of other people were saying the same thing to Mum. On a deep level, after all the battles with school, she'd always believed that if she said to me, 'I don't want you to do it,' it wouldn't make any difference anyway – she was of the unshakeable opinion: 'James always does what he wants to do.' But this time, she suddenly thought, 'They're right. I need to say, "Don't do it."' And that was the first time she directly pleaded with me to stop.

This was just before I was about to fly out to Ukraine, and the film shot by Channel 4 on the train journey where Mum is asking me not to do it any more is real. She was very worried about Mustang, that he was 'not all there'; she was also concerned about the crazy special police in Kiev. And at that point she didn't really know Alex, the film director. She said: 'These people don't care if you fall off, James. They'll have great footage anyway. You need to think about what you're doing here. I'm asking you to stop.'

Nowadays Mum loves Alex. He's a really nice dude, a good mate (especially after everything we went through in Kiev) and he stuck to his word: he told Mum before any filming began that he wouldn't encourage me to do anything stupid, or anything I didn't feel comfortable doing. Even if I didn't climb anything at all, Channel 4 would still produce the film. Alex wasn't interested in making a cheap, sensational film about a nut-job. By witnessing Mustang's antics at close-hand, the idea was more to get me to see how things might appear through Mum's eyes. That sort of worked.

But Mum's pleading didn't make any difference, of course. Except that it perhaps de-stressed her a bit. She'd finally said exactly what she'd meant to say: that she wanted me to stop. Those were a very long 10 or 12 days for her to get through. Then, of course, I went straight back to Kiev – this time without the security blanket of Alex and the film crew.

Mum takes confidence from my background in parkour; she knows my balance is great, that my movement is good and fluid, my grip strong. And I'm always telling her, 'I'm not going up there to die. I want to live. I'm going up there to enjoy it, I'm good at what I do.' I think I can convince her even though she's always like, 'You never really know, James – the wind might blow, there might be a seagull . . .'

• • •

MUM TAKES CONFIDENCE FROM MY BACKGROUND IN PARKOUR

There's another sequence in *Don't Look Down* where I have to abandon a climb. Normally, if it's raining, you can make it up the ladder, even walk out onto the beam of a crane just fine. In the rain, everything has to be slowed down a bit – it's still easy, just not so enjoyable: you really have to concentrate on each movement. Part of the fun of being up there is to move about freely, to jump and mess about on the arm, check out the view and the birds – whereas in the rain it all becomes a bit more like brain surgery. I'll sometimes check the weather forecast beforehand – it's nice to be forewarned, but you can never trust the weather in the UK. Occasionally it looks dry, but then you get up the crane and it's dewy – that sucks! When you're not on solid ground, when you're isolated in the air, you can smell the weather – you can smell the rain coming in. Sometimes I can be driving somewhere and I can feel the weather turning, and I'll think, 'Ah, fuck it, I can't be arsed,' then I'll turn round and go home. But if some filming has been planned . . . well, sometimes you just have to go ahead.

It was dry at first, the morning I attempted to climb up the red crane in Southampton harbour, late 2014, for Channel 4. I'd really wanted to do that crane for a long time, and the camera crew were all down – everyone was here. I'd got my mate Spencer up at the crack of dawn to drive me and Alex to the waterfront. It was completely my decision to go ahead, though – I was under no pressure at all from Alex or Channel 4 (that was the deal for the documentary). But once I'd snuck into the site and got higher up the ladder, I could feel the mist in the air and I could tell the rain was coming. Then the police arrived, and I thought, 'Fuck it, I'm down.' It just wasn't meant to be. But we got some quite cool interaction with the police on film. And Spencer was great on camera. He's an old parkour mate, one of my best mates – but he doesn't climb much, he's scared of heights. And, as he said in the film, he promised his mum he wouldn't do it. He's comfortable on the roof of Burger King, but up a crane is something else. A lot of people are like that: fine on a rooftop, even though climbing up a crane is far more straightforward and probably far less dangerous than being on a roof.

In the UK you have to do climbs in the spring or summer – when the sun comes out super-early, and you've got time to chill out high up somewhere before people start travelling to work. May or June is peak time for climbing and shooting videos at 4 a.m. That was just like it was when me and Spencer did the disused gas-holder near St Mary's Stadium, Southampton's football ground.

The gas-holder itself had been dismantled a few years earlier, but the frame – the same as those anywhere across the country, like the famous ones by the Oval cricket ground – was still in place. It's a beautiful metal, circular structure. Scanning the city skyline as I always did, I was aware of its presence. Myself and Spence used to hang around there, taking pictures of the shell of the gas-holder silhouetted against the sunset.

One night, Spencer stayed over in Romsey and we drove out to St Mary's early in the morning. We snuck into the gas works over a sharp fence then jumped between several pipes, balancing along some of them. I climbed straight up the side of one of the metal beams. It was a super-easy climb, even for Spence, who took the ladder. I went up the outside girders all the way to the top. We walked all the way around the circumference of the holder just as the sun was coming up, at about 4:30 or 5 o'clock in the morning. Because it was a disused gas works we didn't have to worry about people arriving for work. We sat there for a while, and we could see the traffic building in town, people beginning to make their way to their jobs. It wasn't the most spectacular view, to be honest, as we were only 30 metres in the air, nearly 100 feet off the ground. We got some nice photos, even though we couldn't quite see the pitch of St Mary's.

My mate Zeff is another lovely dude. Zeff Harris – cool name, and not a negative bone in his body. By day he works as a carpenter, by night Zeff is a drum and bass producer. Back in 2013, before he became the dad of two lovely little kids, I'd turn up at his house at about 10 o'clock and we'd sit up all night. I'd be editing a film of some climb or jumps, or some rooftop action, and while I was doing that Zeff would be making a track to accompany it.

But perhaps not the sort of track many people would think – for some reason people always want to know about the adrenaline. When I'm at the top of a crane, I'm not convulsing to a 150bpm techno track pumping through my head. It's the opposite, really. I'm totally calm; I've got beautiful ambient music floating through my head. At the top of the Southampton crane, as the sun comes up above the harbour, I wanted a soundtrack that was calming and uplifting, but also a bit moody. Myself and Zeff put it together pretty fast. I need the music to fit what's going on in my head . . . I don't usually want a song, I just need an atmospheric soundtrack, a sound design that follows the film and brings everything to life. Working with Zeff is one of my rare cases of delegation – it's true, I am a bit of a perfectionist.

As we set off on the morning of the aborted climb in Southampton, Alex got into the back of the car to film me and Spencer and he was amazed at how calm we both were. We weren't yelling at each other, hyping each other up into some kind of mad frenzy of peak adrenaline rush. Parkour is a very precise art – you've got to calmly focus on things like distance, and mental attitude has to be perfect. You can't afford to have a mishap because you're too excited. Parkour teaches you that if you're scared or jumpy, you're way more at risk. But if you're calm, you can reach any height safely. Nowadays, I'm always really calm, never more so than at the top of a crane.

6

CALIFORNIA, BIRDS, INDIA

MOST PEOPLE IN THE PARKOUR WORLD KNOW EACH OTHER

The Sepulveda Dam is a huge drainage channel that diverts winter floodwater along the Los Angeles river in the San Fernando Valley. It's a famous location, mainly from featuring in plenty of 1960s Hollywood films (usually at the climax of a tense car chase), and movies like *Iron Man* and *Escape from New York*, as well as TV shows like *Knight Rider*. A heavily moustachioed Lee Majors, the Six Million Dollar Man, once sprinted across the vast smooth white expanse of concrete in an open-necked shirt and tight slacks in order to spot-kick a smoking radioactive device over the top of the dam into the water the other side, where it could presumably safely explode, a major flood and nuclear catastrophe narrowly averted.

It's one hell of a place to skate, and make a tree-running film. I went there with my mate Josh. We skated, ran and jumped across bridge struts until the sun went down. Whenever I've got some new footage, I look through it then go through some of the music people have sent me. For this short film I wanted a steady soundtrack – hip-hop beats and ambient noise, no lyrics, nothing in your face, just something right for chillin' in a concrete playground, chucking tumbleweed into a channel.

Climbing the bridges there, they were full of shit: thick cobwebs, bats' nests and spiders. That reminded me a bit of India. Naturally, coming across birds' nests is a bit of an occupational hazard for me. Back in the UK, I've been attacked by seagulls at that time in the season when their eggs are in the nest, and the seagulls swoop down and catch your head – just to give you a warning.

In India, eagles are the equivalent of seagulls and pigeons – in fact, they *eat* the pigeons. Eagles are everywhere in the sky there. I was once attacked by an eagle on a rooftop in Bangalore; its wingspan must have been a metre and a half across. I was back down on the ground fairly sharpish – it was scary, but pretty cool.

● ● ●

I was in Bangalore doing a job for a well-established parkour performance team I knew, a group of people in Basingstoke called 3Run. Most people in the parkour world know each other; it's a small world. Me and Danny knew them and had worked with them before. 3Run phoned up, and the job was for 12 days of performances in India. A construction company had developed some flat-pack houses – a lot of people are still in need of basic housing in India, obviously – from housing kits that were fairly cheap to make and super-easy to put together. They were sort of modern-day, prefabricated IKEA-like homes. We were flying out to Bangalore to perform some parkour for a promotional film on the roofs of their flat-pack builds. So we spent a couple of days shooting a video, leaping between concrete slabs and across roofs. The prefabs held up well enough.

From the hotel we were staying in we'd seen this massive crane in the distance. All the guys were all saying, 'James, you're the crane guy. When are you going to do that?'

WHEREVER I AM IN THE WORLD, I'M USUALLY WALKING AROUND LOOKING UP AT THE SKYLINE

So I got up about 4 a.m. one morning before work. There was security everywhere on the building site. I had to choose my moment, jump over this fence, drop into a gap at the back of some toilets then crawl along by these corrugated portaloos – they fucking stank! Made of metal corrugated sheets, they were held together by wood, true Indian-style. It was just getting light, and I could make out the bodies of dead dogs lying around. A pretty desolate shit-hole – if there'd been a river there you'd have seen a body floating past.

It's never quiet in Bangalore – even at five in the morning there are people everywhere, horns going beep-beep, animals making a racket. Somehow I managed to evade security – which was quite a feat, given the number of people walking around in hi-visibility jackets, talking loudly. I leapt across a few newly constructed concrete walls and slipped into the shell of the tower block that was being constructed, then walked up some basic stairs to reach the bottom of the crane, the tallest of three.

'Same old crane,' I thought, 'but perhaps a different view.' Actually, as soon as I started climbing, I realised there was a layer of dripped concrete globules, sort of rough gobbets of building material on just about every girder of the crane, coating each rung of the ladder – certainly lower down. They were really sharp; I couldn't have done that climb barefoot. As I climbed, the sun broke across the horizon. I could see water down below, some kind of lake – I'm not sure how fresh it was. And there were slums everywhere. There was our nice hotel to one side, but the other shore of the lake looked pretty rough and run-down, really poor. But the coloured buildings – pale blue, lime green and yellow – looked incredibly beautiful from above.

I'd climbed up 75 metres or so, did the usual crane stuff: walked the length of the arm, hung off the end of it. In the film, as I dangle, you can see a lump of grease and shit all over my hand. Even that early in the morning there was a slight haze building in the air. The soundtrack to the film is a touch Indian-sounding, with sitars accompanying the bit where I'm jumping around the walls to get to the crane, before that drops out and Zeff builds up a calming and relaxing drone – which is perfect for the sense of bliss up there at the top.

Wherever I am in the world, I'm usually walking around looking up at the skyline, checking for cranes and unfinished buildings. Failing that, I'm sitting right at the top of a crane, looking down. In Bangalore, perched on the edge of that filthy crane, I could see the building-site workers scuttling about 250 feet or so below. It really felt as it had atop plenty of other cranes in other cities – like us humans, we're really nothing more than tiny grains of sand on the infinite beach of the universe.

SOUTH BANK TOWER, TRAINERS, NEAR MISS ON THE ROOF OF A CHINESE TAKE-AWAY, DON'T JUDGE ME

Climbing cranes and hanging off them is not really about strength, it's not really about muscle either – it's all about control, plus the various techniques which you can't get without years of parkour training. For instance, learning how to take off and land properly, and how to execute various other techniques. It looks simple but when you actually try it, the agility needed and the spatial awareness – you don't get those without endless practice. Because I've been doing it for so long I can jump rooftops better than some people can jog. I know plenty of people who are conventionally strong, but put them on a wall and tell them to jump a gap, and they'll say, 'Er, how do I do this? How should I swing my arms?'

I WAS ON HIGH ALERT FOR CRANES

I WAS HANGING OFF THE EDGE OF THE ROOF WITH MY RIGHT HAND

I CAN ONLY REALLY PUT MY TRUST IN MYSELF

I don't go to the gym, or have a special diet. I like cashew nuts, and I generally eat healthily. My muscle memory is good, and I keep my technique topped up with the occasional session up on the roof of Burger King – that keeps me in good enough shape.

I find myself talking about this sort of thing all of the time, my mind wandering in various meetings. On one such occasion I was talking to a TV production company while gazing out across the Thames, scanning the riverbank for development, when I spotted a pretty tall crane, 170 metres maybe, which was lifting concrete blocks that would form the South Bank Tower, just by the Southbank Centre.

Around this time, spring 2014, I was on high alert for cranes. That evening I was still up in London, hanging out with a friend of mine. We decided to get into the site and climb to the rooftop of the partially constructed tower, but not the actual crane. She bloody loved it, was up for it; but I checked out the crane at close quarters and made a mental note to revisit the site to shoot a video.

A few weeks later, three of us stayed in London one Saturday night then rode across town on Boris bikes to the site, weaving across empty roads at 3:30 on a Sunday morning, on what was a good half-hour cycle ride.

It was super-easy to get into the site early on a Sunday morning – security were dozing in a cabin. We hopped over a wall, sneaked around and found the stairs all the way to the roof. From there it was a simple hop across to the crane. Despite the steep angle of the arm of the crane, it was an easy climb – up the ladders, then up the arm. It was a perfect morning. The sun had just come up, and I could see the shadow cast by The Shard across the Thames and the residential housing of the South Bank. The view across London was simply mind-boggling, the blazing sun burning off the haze, lighting up the city from above the Thames to the west.

• • •

When I'm not fielding questions about fitness regimes and diet, I'm responding to enquiries about the trainers I wear. There's no big secret there, either: I need a pair that are practical and cool at the same time. I've never really made a big deal out of trainers, but everybody else seems to – a lot of newbies to parkour are obsessed by this. It's true; I usually appear in the same model of trainers in all my films. DC is an American skate brand; they've got a trainer with the soft sole of normal running trainers, squidgy and rubbery. People struggle to understand that it doesn't really matter. The best shoe, for grip and all-round feel, is no shoe at all – barefoot. For little technical things, balancing barefoot is the best. Your feet are extensions of your

hands, your toes grip a rail, you sink into it; you grab it with your feet. I'd do more stuff barefoot, but you can't jump as far, or do as many jumps; there's not much protection. That bit of natural padding on your feet can't take that much – the initial impact hurts if you don't have trainers on.

DCs – I like the way they look, but most running trainers are the same, really. You don't want anything lumpy, it has to be a smooth piece of rubber, like a tyre – the best tyres have nothing but slick rubber slits – well, pure rubber, but with a bit of texture in there to help you get a grip. I once got hold of a job lot of DC trainers when they were just being discontinued – I brought ten pairs back from California. I've still got loads of brand-new pairs underneath the stairs in every single possible colour, but trainers are not particularly important, any old running shoe will do.

The finest trainers in the world won't save you if something goes wrong. For me, something going wrong is down to preparation or the materials being out of my control. As I've said, I can only really put my trust in myself, and in materials that I'm happy will bear my weight. Once, Gibbs and Doug and I were out on a night mission in Southampton. We were exploring a new circuit, jumping about on the roofs of some offices and flats, the backs of shops and stuff, not far from

my flat near the waterfront. We found ourselves on a series of descending roofs and ended up balancing across the tip of these tiled roofs, then sliding down the tiles to the edge that overhangs the street below. That was quite a dodgy moment: you had to stop yourself before the gutter and then drop down to the rooftop below. We worked down several rooftops like that, and the last roof in that row was about a 5-metre, 16-foot drop – a bit of a leap. We were doing this quite fast, with no real idea of what was going to happen next, but we were all capable on roofs, and we thought, 'Ah, fuck it, if we get stuck, we'll deal with it. We're not that high, we'll figure something out.' And so we dropped down onto the last roof, and we were looking around. Then it dawned: 'Fuck it, there's no way down either side!' We were suddenly stuck, stranded on this roof. But over one side of the building there was an overhang of about 2 feet, three stories above the street, which was a bit too far to drop. Underneath the overhang was a drainpipe. I manoeuvred myself to hang onto the edge of the overhang to see if I could reach the drainpipe to test it to see if it was strong enough to take our weight. It was a metal drainpipe, which was a good start – not the plastic rubbish you find on most new-builds – but I could also see that it was old and a bit rusty.

So I was hanging off the edge of the roof with my right hand, just about touching the top of the drainpipe with my left, but because I was so far away from it I couldn't really get any force to shake it properly. So I just thought, 'Fuck it,' and let go. I came off the roof and put both hands on the pipe and prayed. But as soon as I put my second hand and full weight onto the drainpipe it made an awful creaking noise, and started to come away from the wall. I began falling backwards, desperately clutching onto the pipe – I don't think I had time to ponder any profound thoughts about mortality before the pipe sort of buckled and became stuck in its hinge, about 10 feet below. It had come about 2 feet away from the wall, then suddenly swung around in the hinge and slammed me into the upstairs windowsill of the Chinese takeaway next door.

I managed to squeeze myself into this windowsill and hold on. At least the windowsill was big enough, so I could relax. But then I realised I couldn't sit up there until daybreak. I'd have to hang off the ledge and just take the drop – there was a big dumpster with one of those soft plastic, bendy covers over it. I let go of the sill and fell about 15 feet onto the bin, but it was fine because it was so soft. Doug, who was laughing on the roof, threw me his car keys and I walked round back into the street and got his bag out of the car. He had a slackline, which is like an industrial-sized ratchet-strap (the sort of thing you use to strap luggage onto the roof of a car). It was a nice solid nylon strap, 25 metres long, and Doug and Gibbs used that to climb down the roof. It was 3 a.m., the Chinese restaurant and takeaway was closed, so no one saw us climb down, get in the car and head off home.

CLIMBING HIGH CRANES IS JUST MY WAY OF DOING THINGS

Some people – the ones who yell 'Spiderman' out of passing vans – would probably say being stuck on the roof of a Chinese was the least I deserved. But most people, 99 per cent, I'd say, love what I do and send in messages on Facebook every day. That said, it's the 1 per cent who tend to stick with you. Sometimes it's hard for people to take me seriously. All they see is the stuff I do, and to them it's mental. But they don't know anything about me: my thoughts, my motivation; my background, my training. I always get one interviewer who'll pipe up with something like, 'You're encouraging kids to go out and take risks, and that's bad.' No, I'm not here to encourage that. Climbing high cranes is just my way of doing things but some people get so annoyed about it. If you stop and think about it, they're actually blaming me for something their kid, or your kid, *might* do. Your kid is your kid because you've made him or her whatever he or she is. If your kid wants to go out and climb a 300-metre crane and hang off it without any thought or practice or training, then he or she must be pretty stupid. I don't think any kid in their right mind would go out and do that. They don't wake up one morning and think, 'Oh, I'll go and hang off a crane today.' And if they do think that, maybe you're doing something wrong as a parent. Kids who do that are not thinking logically or responsibly (school could have also affected their outlook, of course).

But you can't win with some people, they think they're so right. They think I need help, but who's to say what's right and wrong? I dunno, it never ends.

What I do think is anything's possible if you put your mind to it. As I've said, the adrenaline is not really pumping when I'm up somewhere. I'm calm and in control, seeing the bigger picture, seeing everything for what it is – the specks of life below. There's a certain freedom to that. I live for the moment and take things as they come. Not knowing what's around the corner keeps me on my toes. If you're living something you've already done, you know exactly what's going to happen next. Is that really living?

THE
EIFFEL
TOWER

Every year some friends and I would go on a tour with a couple of vans – one was an old converted fire truck with beds in it. We'd start off in Liverpool, drive down through London, pick up some people then drive on through Europe to beautiful places like the Alps. In October 2014 we'd just finished one of these trips, ending up in Copenhagen. By that point Stevy and I couldn't face the 12-hour drive home in the cramped, hot van, so we just decided to go somewhere on the spur of the moment. Paris was easy and cheap, just an hour and a half away. I'd been in Denmark with my friend Danny and also his younger brother Stevy. They're a real parkour family, naturally amazing at stuff like that – Stevy is just like a smaller version of Danny. Both have hands like elephant hide; really thick skin, proper workers' hands, really solid. Stevy is the quieter of the two, but he's as smart and switched on as his brother, and also incredibly capable.

We arrived in the French capital with a rough idea to climb some stuff, take some cool pictures, and make some films – the usual kind of thing. Never once did we think, 'We'll go to Paris to do the Eiffel Tower.' That felt so out of reach, because it's just. . .well, a special building – you don't really think of climbing things like that.

NEVER ONCE DID WE THINK, 'WE'LL GO TO PARIS TO DO THE EIFFEL TOWER'

So, we were in Paris for a few days. Stevy wanted to explore just as much as I did. We went up the Eiffel Tower – normally, via the lifts and with a bunch of other tourists – and once we were up there, Stevy read my mind. Both of us couldn't help but think, 'This is so easy to climb, it's just a giant ladder.' There's so much of it too – so much metal lattice work to climb up, so many different places to hide – you could climb from the bottom to the very top quite easily, with not much skill and with a fair chance of not being seen. 'Since we're here, we might as well give it a go,' we reckoned.

So we came up with a plan to take the very last lift up in the evening and then, when it was closing time, to take the stairs back down . . . You can take the lift to the very top, to the birdcage platform, but you can only take the stairs to the second viewing platform, effectively about halfway up. They've blocked the stairs off from there because as you go up, they narrow into a tighter spiral with no safety barriers and you wouldn't want tourists staggering up and down them. So, in our plan, once the very last lift had gone we thought it would be really easy to hang around the stairs until it was quiet, then just climb into the framework somewhere between the first and second platforms, hide for a bit, wait for it to completely die down and empty out, then we'd come out and climb all the way back up again – on the outside.

That was the idea, but we found way too many security people working there, clearing everyone out from the middle staircase, running up and down the stairs to get all the visitors out as quickly as possible so they could go home. We hung around, but they weren't having it: 'We are closing, you need to leave,' they told us, so we just left.

We were walking away from one of the legs where you come out.

'So, plan B,' I said.

'We don't really have a plan B,' Stevy pointed out.

'Well, why don't we just try to climb it from the floor, straight up the sides?' I suggested. 'If we do get caught, at least we'll get caught fairly low down, and not at the top – and we won't get into as much trouble, probably.'

Stevy was up for it.

Every night, on the hour, the tower sparkles – lit up by 20,000 light bulbs. One corner by one of the legs was cordoned off by a 10-foot fence where there was some construction work going on. We hopped over the fence and suddenly we were looking up at this huge leg of the tower. There were three cameras on each face of the leg – two either side, pointing inwards, and one in the middle, pointing straight down. My first thought was, 'Not a chance!

There's cameras everywhere – everything is covered.' Then, during the last sparkle show at 1 a.m., I had a sudden revelation: I knew these CCTV cameras were likely to be low-quality with exposure that adjusts to the current lighting conditions so if you were to put sparkling light in front of an automatic camera, it'd freak the hell out. Any security guards watching at such a moment wouldn't be able to see anything – or, at best, all they'd catch would be a few moments of flashing white light.

'Stevy, quick, if we're going to do this, we should do it now,' I told him. We thought we'd get a reasonable way up the leg while the light show was still flashing. The second we got on it, it actually stopped – '*Fuck!*' But we carried on anyway, on the outside corner of the leg, and 10 seconds later we were above the cameras.

We climbed up for about another 20 metres, got to the point where the legs join the main structure, and just sat there for a bit, cleared our heads and tried not to get too carried away. By then we were about a third of the way up, roughly 100 feet, and no one had seen us yet – it was unreal! We sat there for a few minutes. The workers were still cleaning the staircases and the first viewing platform, but it was dark and we were hidden in the ironwork at the back. There was just parkland, the Champ de Mars, out of the back corner where we were perched, but no one was having a picnic at 1:30 in the morning, so we climbed a bit further out, scaled

the outside of the tower and got back in just above the second platform. We were looking down on all the closed restaurants and you could see security guards walking around with torches. We discovered a ladder that ran up the inside of a lift shaft before we came across the cordoned-off stairs and made our way to the top.

There's a door at the top of the stairs leading to the top platform. In the daytime the door is manned, but at this point we got carried away. There didn't seem to be anyone around, although the lights were still on, and there were cameras everywhere, so we just pressed the button of the electromagnetic door to the top platform and went in. As soon as we stepped into the room a walkie-talkie went crazy, just exploded in a cacophony of voices and static. I practically shat myself. My heart was pounding and it took me a panicky second to realise there wasn't anyone actually there – it was just a radio. Even so, while my French isn't good, I had the feeling we'd been rumbled. Stevy was at the top of the stairs behind me – we legged it back down about five flights.

As we descended each level, I could see through the lattice work that, on two opposite corners where the beams were huge, there were hollows, square gaps with small flat floors – sort of pots that got bigger the lower you went. Eventually we reached a pair you could climb into. Stevy is tiny, skinny and double-jointed, so I said, 'Stevy, just go over there, climb in the hole

and I'll come and get you when it's clear.' By this point the lifts were firing up. You could see the cables moving; hear keys jangling, people shouting. So we leapt into opposite pots. Someone was running up the stairs, walkie-talkies were crackling.

I'm much bigger than Stevy so I had to take my shoe off, get one leg in the pot first and then rest my knee on the shoe and crouch in a position as if I were poised on the blocks for a 100-metre sprint. My head was sticking out a tiny bit, but there wasn't much I could do about that.

I did fully poke my head out a couple of times and I saw people with torches, but there was so much to the tower the chances of them seeing us were quite low. This went on till about 2:30 or 3 o'clock. Forty-five minutes or so is quite a long time to remain completely still, crouched on one leg. Then suddenly there was nothing: the walkie-talkies stopped, the stairway fell silent. It all went dead. They knew we were there, but perhaps by this point they thought we'd just jumped off with parachutes – they've had a lot of base-jumpers do that from the Eiffel Tower.

It stayed quiet for a while, but I had to move. By then I was in agony – my leg was completely numb; I was bent in such an uncomfortable position. 'Please, let this be it,' I whimpered to myself. Everything stayed quiet.

As soon as I put my head out of the hole, the whole fucking tower lit up. Every one of those 20,000 lights suddenly seemed to be burning at full wattage. It went nuts: the lifts burst into life and I could hear walkie-talkies again, guards shouting and running up and down the staircase.

I went straight back into the hole for what felt like another agonising two hours. Somehow, they still didn't spot us. So I chanced sticking my head up a few more times, shifted about to beat the cramp in my legs and the pain in my back, and slowly the voices quietened down, then finally once more the lights went off. I got out, crept around a bit to get the blood flowing again, and went over to see Stevy. He was asleep! Snug in his pot, being so tiny and skinny and double-jointed, he could fold up in there like a human garden chair.

We laughed as we realised the tower was ours again, but this time we thought we'd leave the top platform alone – we could go up there any time in the day anyhow. Instead we decided to aim for just below the top platform, to climb up the outer edge, working our way up the beams on the outside. We went up; we came down. We just hung around up there, sitting on the girders as a grey, peaceful dawn began to break over Paris. You get different vibes from different cities – different smells, ambience and street noise. Paris in the very early morning, or late at night, is just amazing – you can feel it, so nice and relaxed, so much love. It's quite a romantic place; people are loved-up.

Around 7 o'clock, the lifts suddenly came on again. We assumed it would be the workers arriving for the new day, and shot back into a couple of those pots, midway between the second and third platforms. But from my hole, now it was light, I could see through the Perspex screen of the lifts that they were empty. I watched a few go by, just getting used to the fact that there was no one in them.

Once the light was good we could film a bit more. I had the camera strapped on my head – of course, the pictures are better when it's in your mouth (and anything physical, flipping or jumping, has to be filmed from your mouth), but when you're climbing the Eiffel Tower you need to be able to breathe and speak.

After being folded up in one of those pots for a few hours, getting my body moving again got some of the other temporarily suspended processes to fire back up, and I was called up to take a leak quite urgently. I try to keep a level head while on a climb, but there's just something about being up on such an iconic monument – it had to be off the edge of it!

We hung around up there, just chillin' and gazing over the city for another couple of hours, but the whole escapade finished with us being caught, taken down and arrested. We climbed down to a maintenance platform to meet the workers who'd spotted us, and they escorted us down to the ground floor in a lift. The doors opened and there were about ten police, all armed with guns, to greet us. But they were actually really nice, just doing their job. Professionally, their line was a stern: 'You shouldn't do this.' But then, personally, they couldn't help but be interested: 'How was it? How the *fuck* did you do that?' It was all pretty intriguing to them because it was so out of their zone.

AS SOON AS I PUT MY HEAD OUT OF THE HOLE, THE WHOLE FUCKING TOWER LIT UP

They took us in the back of a police car to a police station about a five-minute drive away. Once there, we were handcuffed to some benches for an hour or two. Occasionally, someone would come out. Once, they took our bags to search them. Up on the tower, as soon as I knew that we'd been seen, and that we'd have no choice but to surrender ourselves, I took all the SD cards out of my cameras. I had three cameras on me: my Cannon 5-D Mark 3 (a massive DSLR) and two GoPros and the phone as well. So I hid the SD cards in a tiny little slit in my backpack, a long, slim pen pocket – I stuffed them down to the bottom of there. At the police station they came back in with the bags: 'You've got three cameras in here. Show us your footage,' a policeman said.

'Oh, I didn't film anything,' I replied. 'My batteries died in one camera, and I forgot my SD cards too.'

'OK, what about your phone? Is there anything on there?'

'Yeah, there's some stuff – loads, in fact – on my phone.'

So I had to delete everything on my phone. I dunno why, really – a security breach, or something. But it worked out really well. That was kind of dummy footage, and I was trying not to laugh about the real footage stuffed down my backpack – I think the phone kind of distracted them from my cameras. I was amazed we got away with that. On the phone there was some good stuff filmed from where I was hiding in the hole – footage of the security guards searching for us, waving torchlights around and yelling into walkie-talkies. It was a shame I had to delete all of that, but I got to keep the rest.

When they left us alone again, I whispered to Stevy: 'The SD cards are still here!' We were super-excited the cards were still in the bag. But then suddenly I felt a chill down my spine. They'd asked me about the footage, and I'd denied we had anything, but then it dawned on me that they might have got hold of the SD cards anyway, copied the contents and be searching through them on their computers at that very moment, so they'd know I'd clearly lied to them. I was still worrying about that when they took us into separate rooms to question us individually.

WHO WAS I? WHY DID I DO THIS? HOW DID I DO THIS?

The policewoman who interviewed me was really cool. Her first question was: 'How the fuck did you do that? And how did you get past security?' Then she laughed, and before I could answer properly, she said she was shit-scared of heights and couldn't believe we'd climbed the tower. Her second question was: 'Did you leave a bomb up there?' This time I laughed and then she was laughing again – she was cool, you could joke with her. She knew we weren't actual terrorists, she knew we were just messing around, but she had to follow a script. They always jump straight to the terrorist thing. It was the same with the manager of the Moscow Bridge in Kiev – he was worried we'd left explosives up there. Ukraine is an edgy place, I guess, but a lot of people are brainwashed into that kind of thinking. Terrorism is what everybody wants us to be scared of, isn't it?

The policewoman in Paris followed up with a few normal questions – who was I? Why did I do this? How did I do this (again)? I told her pretty much everything about our night up the tower, but not about the CCTV cameras and the lights.

Usually police the world over wade in with the same scare tactics at first: 'You could go to jail', 'You could get fined up to 10,000 Euros', 'You could be deported'. And I always stay calm: I'm thinking, 'OK, you can be angry, but that's not going to change me, or who I am in this moment, or what I've done. You might threaten me with a fine, but I'm still comfortable in this situation. I'm not going to break down and start crying.' I don't know what they want, really – what they expect with that aggressive approach. It doesn't work on me; I'm not scared by police at all, I couldn't care less. I've had enough run-ins with them here in the UK, and in Europe. I'm really not fussed any more, and eventually they can see that. Then sometimes they try to scare you even more – like the German cop in Marktoberdorf (see Chapter 10). Once they've tried to scare you, they gauge how you react to things. They have a set bunch of questions, they see how you react and then that influences how they treat you. It's a sort of test they base their judgement on.

It was the policewoman who'd made me delete the phone footage, and one of her colleagues had been full-on with the scare tactics: 'prison' – sure; 'a fine' – OK; I didn't really believe any of it. I was a first-time offender (on French soil), and there had been no criminal damage. Then the policewoman returned to asking me about where the gap in security was.

Maybe because it was the Eiffel Tower, or perhaps the scare tactics were working, after all, but suddenly I became a bit on edge: could they really do us for this in the modern-day world of terror threats? (At least this was October 2014, a year before things became really jumpy in Paris.) Could they jail us to set an example, as they tend to do in the States? I asked her if we were going to get into massive trouble. She said she didn't know. So I proposed a deal: I would tell the policewoman how to make the tower impossible to climb if she would let us go. That wasn't really down to her, she told me, but she left the room to speak to her colleagues.

She returned and said they'd phoned up a judge right there and then. A few minutes later the judge phoned back and it transpired we were OK: we could go as long as we signed a document saying we wouldn't climb the tower again for a period of three years. We'd effectively been issued with a restraining order on the Eiffel Tower and the policewoman never followed up on my ideas for improving security. I guess she didn't really care – I suppose it was not her concern, ultimately . . .

DUBAI
CRANE

450 METRES REMAINS THE BIGGEST ONE I'VE DONE

By the marina in Dubai, they're erecting the world's tallest residential building – they're still doing it now. I clocked it when I first got there – you couldn't really miss it, it was fucking huge. It was ridiculously high – 450 metres, or something. I thought, 'Yeah, I'll just try it. I'll give it a go.'

I was in Dubai in 2014, shooting a music video. The brief for the job was straightforward: 'Climb something, send us some footage.' It was for a house and drum and bass producer called Redlight. I went to shoot that and then hung around for a couple of weeks. That's what I always do: do the job, then hang out with mates.

Anyhow, I woke up at 4:30 a.m., got a taxi from the hotel – that cost about 80p, it's so cheap out there – and then tried to find a way in. The problem with Dubai is that because of the heat the workers get to work around 4 a.m. So I had to hop over this fence and about 10 metres away was this coach, full of workers, people getting off and heading into work. I had to crawl across the ground alongside a pile of scaffolding poles to the base of the crane. The crane went all the way from the floor, the full 450 metres up the side of the building. When the workers disappeared into the building, I started to climb up the crane. That was pretty straightforward – for about 50 metres. Then I realised I had my full-on backpack on. This was Dubai – 30 degrees even at 4 a.m. I had one tiny

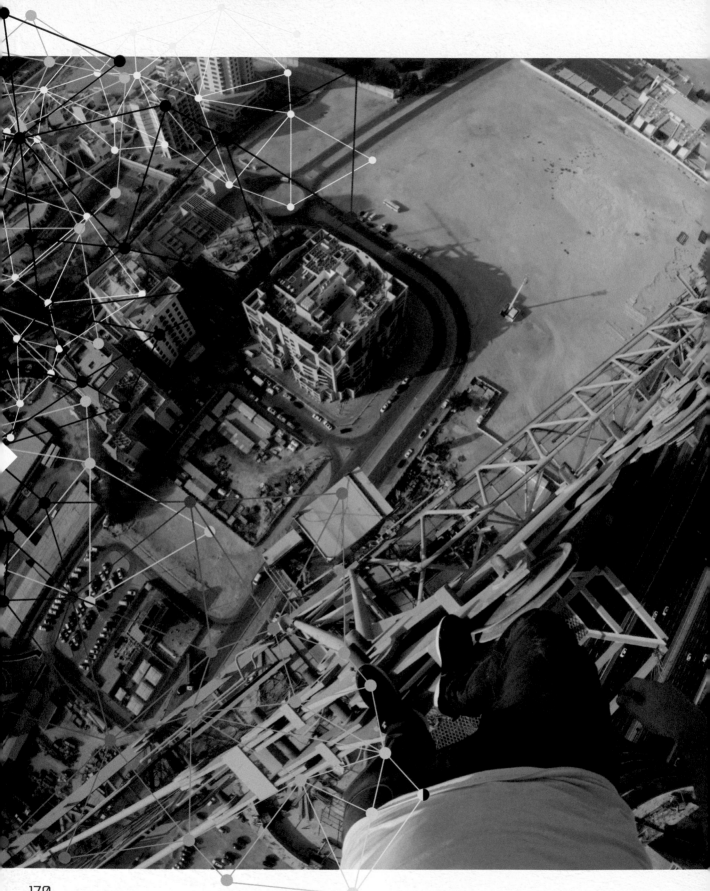

bottle of water, and it was super-dry and dusty on the building site. Already I was dying, so I went in and found the stairs and started walking up. That took bloody ages! I bumped into some people, they shook my hand – 'Good morning' and all the rest of it – they had no idea who I was.

Walking up stairs is far more of a hassle than climbing a crane. About 120 stories later, exhausted, I finally made it out onto the roof. The sun was coming up. I worked my way round to a metal platform, a sort of walkway, from where I could jump onto the crane.

This was a really steep crane – but cranes are the same the world over, even in Dubai – a huge yellow ladder, basically. Once I was on it, I realised it was a bit greasy, but the view climbing past the driver's cab was special: the tower blocks of Dubai at dawn, including the dome of the world's previous tallest building; the yellow threads of fluorescent light from the still-lit motorways; the stylised palm-tree shape of Palm Jumeirah, an artificial archipelago, and the surrounding deep, peaceful aquamarine of the Persian Gulf. The most beautiful sunrise imaginable began to spread from the east; it took the edge off the blinding flash of the red aeroplane light at the very top of the crane.

I was sitting at the top, just looking at the marina below, enjoying the calm and the sunrise, when all of a sudden the crane started powering up, the cables began spinning and the arm started to twist around. 'What the fuck!' I climbed down 30 metres or so to the cabin (thankfully, he was a pretty smooth crane-operator), opened the door and the driver was in there. He seemed pleasant enough, and we started having a little chat. He was just smiling; he looked happy, he wasn't scared – even with this strange dude suddenly appearing in his cab at 5 o'clock in the morning, 400 metres in the air.

Once we'd established I'd been sitting at the very top when he'd powered up the crane, I asked him if it was OK to go back up for a bit. He took a picture of me, and agreed not to move it while I went up. I think he just thought, 'Fuckin' hell, he's come all this way, I'll let him go to the top.' But he must have been shitting himself.

It was the greasiest crane I'd ever seen – that didn't really bother me; it just meant I had to slow down a bit, take it steady, get my feet in the right spot and hook my legs round a few bars. The sun was incredible. It was fully light by the time I was back up at the top, the view was awesome . . . I just enjoyed the moment – when you're climbing you don't really

WHEN YOU'RE CLIMBING YOU DON'T REALLY THINK ABOUT ANYTHING OTHER THAN BEING IN THAT PARTICULAR MOMENT

think about anything other than being in that particular moment, the calm, blissful state you're in. Then, like every other time, I started thinking, 'I'm super-thirsty here, very dehydrated – starving too. What am I going to have for breakfast?'

Other people, some of the workers, had seen me up there by this time. I climbed down and got caught, inevitably. People came up and met me and took me right down to the ground – 'Please don't do that again.' I was mostly worried for the crane-driver. He could have been asked why he wasn't moving the crane. But Dubai is

not like the rest of the world – the police there are different, for a start. Well, in truth, the police aren't very often involved. If the building-site workers had phoned the police they'd have all lost their jobs. I'd have been OK, I wouldn't get into trouble, but they'd all be out of work, so they tend not to phone the police, which is good. It frustrates me sometimes when they talk to me like I'm a child, but I'm happy that security in Dubai remains pretty relaxed.

450 metres remains the biggest crane I've done – I'd happily do that one again.

WALKING UP STAIRS
IS FAR MORE OF
A HASSLE THAN
CLIMBING A CRANE

GERMANY, ITALY

10

In the autumn of 2014, my director Alex and I toured *Don't Look Down* around several cities in Germany as part of the European Outdoor Film Tour. We'd had about 600 people turn up in Munich for the first date. After the screening we did a kind of question and answer session (a fair few of the audience seemed interested to know what trainers I wore). We were driving on our way to the next date, in Füssen in southwest Bavaria, home to the spectacular Neuschwanstein Castle, when I caught sight of a huge chimney in the Marktoberdorf area.

The chimney was next to a factory-farming complex of some kind. After I had pulled the hire car over, I was up that chimney. The spiked anti-climbing device – a sort of jagged steel halo around the ladder – was very helpful. It levered me up, gave me something to grab onto; a bit of support. People think, 'Ah, spikes sticking out from a wall: *yeah, this'll get 'em!*' No – this'll help 'em out.

THERE WAS QUITE A BIT OF OUTRAGE ALL TOLD

It was a bit blustery up there but, again, an immense view: the sheds of the farming complex, the sprawl of the town – houses, fields, the countryside stretching all the way to where the low cloud met the horizon. I was on top of the chimney, minding my own business, making echoing noises down the funnel and rotating the GoPro on my extendable selfie stick, when I heard the first wails of sirens.

Alex was sitting in the hire car below. First, the police arrived, then the fire service turned up; then several more police, followed by more fire engines. Then practically the whole village had gathered around the base of the chimney. By that point Alex was sinking lower into the passenger seat of the car. Inevitably the police wandered over and got him to wind down the window.

'Do you know him?' said a cop, gesturing up at the chimney.

'Ah, God, he's not gone up there, has he? You're joking!' protested Alex.

As soon as I was down, I realised I was in a male-female, good cop-bad cop routine again. The man was a complete knob, a total grumpy bastard – I could tell just by the way he looked that he was a dick before he'd even said a word. The woman was really nice. But he spoke and it was the usual: 'You shouldn't be doing this.'

'Yeah, I know. Now what?' I sighed. I was thinking, 'Let's skip the usual bullshit and just cut to the chase.' 'Do you need my details? My passport? What are we doing?' I asked. 'Let's not waste any time. We've got a film to catch – let's just do what we've got to do.'

He immediately said, 'You'll probably need to pay a fine.'

I asked how much.

'I don't know. Come with us.'

I had a sense there was something fishy about this. The car was in my name and they assumed Alex couldn't drive, so they made us follow them in the hire car to a bank. The cop got out of their car and took me into the vestibule of the bank, which was closed – it was late afternoon. 'Put your card in,' he instructed me. I did so, and the display came up – all the options for 10, 20, 40 Euros, right up to 500. I asked again, 'How much is this fine?' In Germany, I think the rule is that you have to pay a certain proportion of your earnings. But the cop just pressed the top number: 500.

'What! This is super-corrupt,' I was thinking.

But the machine didn't work.
He pressed 200.

That didn't work either.

He worked his way right down to 10 Euros. Nothing.

'Funds not available.'

On the journey to the bank, while stationary at a series of traffic lights, I'd logged into my bank on my phone and transferred all the cash in my current account into my savings account. I'd just been paid for a job, so I didn't want to be cleaned out – that would have sucked. I just knew something wasn't right with

I JUST HAD A
SENSE THERE WAS
SOMETHING FISHY
ABOUT THIS

this guy. The first thing he'd mentioned was a fine. I said, 'Oh, right, OK,' but from experience I knew that wasn't how it worked. It's never the first thing the police or security say.

The police guy was so pissed off, though. He was furious. To me it was hilarious.

I shrugged my shoulders and told him: 'I don't have any money.'

He made us get back in the car and follow them to the police station. They needed to process a fine, speak to someone higher up to decide what to do with me – all the usual bullshit. We got there, and they held me for what felt like hours. They put Alex in a separate room – I could see him through the glass. He stood up a few times, made to stretch his legs, as you would after several hours, and every time he did so the policeman on the desk yelled at him to sit down. Alex was getting really pissed off – he doesn't take any shit, he's really cool. He spends much of his life shooting edgy documentaries with difficult tribes in isolated rainforests so he's used to all kinds of bullshit, and some prick behind a desk in a sleepy police station in rural Germany on a quiet Tuesday afternoon was not going to faze him – he hadn't got any time for it. 'Why [can't I walk around]? I haven't done anything wrong. Or are you arresting me now too?' he said. He went ballistic and ended up just walking outside. It was

so stuffy and hot in there. They said to Alex, 'You're either in or out.' He was like, 'Fuck you, I'm gone!'

Eventually the first cop came back into my interview room. 'We've just been on your website. You sell T-shirts and posters and phone cases and stuff, and yet you appear not to have any funds in your bank account.'

'Yeah, it's tough, I don't sell many,' I lied.

'But you need to pay this fine.'

'Yeah, but I can't pay it now. So what do we do?'

I knew they were making it up as they went along too. Corrupt as hell.

So I had to sign something saying I'd climbed the chimney without permission, and they finally let me go. I think they must have got bored of it, realised they were wasting their time, and I never heard anything else.

We made it to the next screening in Füssen just in time. By then we'd hit the news, and as I had some good footage from the GoPro, we decided to include that in the evening's Q&A session. There was quite a bit of outrage all told.

• • •

I'm not so bad at keeping one step ahead of various European police forces, though. Another summer, and another tour – this time in a minibus in 2015 rather than the old fire van – we rolled into Bologna en route from Venice. We'd planned to stop over in an old factory, a sort of abandoned compound made up of industrial flats for former workers and derelict or disused and partly refurbished factories. The whole area was cordoned off by barbed wire, but the building where we were planning to sleep was cool – it was like an indoor gymnasium, with crash mats and bars and all kinds of fun stuff. The tours were getting too big by this point; in fact that was the last one I went on – there were about 30 of us in total, a convoy, and that killed it because it became more like a school trip: really difficult to organise (there aren't too many places willing or able to put up 30-plus parkour dudes) and too structured.

RIGHT OPPOSITE OUR SLEEPING QUARTERS WAS THIS MASSIVE CRANE. I WAS LIKE, 'AH, COME ON'

Right opposite our sleeping quarters was this massive crane. I was like, '*Ah, come on!*' So we just dumped our stuff, snuck off, climbed over a wall and were at the foot of the crane before anyone else managed it – all parkour folk have the same vision at the same time. As soon as we'd trundled into the factory compound and caught sight of the crane we knew we'd all be up there at some point.

It was blisteringly hot, and we'd had to sneak past some security guards with scary-looking beasts – bloody dogs again. We climbed up a few levels on an unfinished building, up some stairs, up a wall, to finally reach the crane, which was sitting on the shell of what looked like it was going to be some kind of car park. It was a hot, dusty afternoon and quite breezy. A fairly windy climb doesn't really make that much difference – only when it comes to balancing on the arm of a crane; obviously then you have to be more careful.

It wasn't the highest crane ever. We went right up the outside of it, then part of a ladder on the inside – the same old trudge up the same old crane design, even in Italy. In fact there was a wider than usual platform at the end of the arm. You could get a nice view of the sunset from there; even as dusk set in and the sun went down there was still a glow, a strange light that made everything slightly unreal and just a bit scary.

We clambered down and were chased by the security guards and the dogs, so we legged it over the barbed wire, crawled through some bushes and made it into the old abandoned apartments – the former living quarters for factory workers. Then we shot out of the back of there and had to climb back over a wall where we'd first been seen before sprinting across a road and back onto the bus. As we slumped into the coach seats we could hear sirens and some police cars flew past. A few other guys from the tour, some Germans, had gone in just after we'd left, and the police grabbed them, mistaking them for us! They hadn't actually been up the crane yet. Good timing for us, bad timing for them…

11
ALMAS TOWER, DUBAI

The moment Philippe Petit, the original *Man on Wire*, stepped out on his tightrope between the Twin Towers in Manhattan in 1974, he wrote in his book, *To Reach the Clouds*: 'All of a sudden the density of the air is no longer the same . . . the horizon is suspended from east to west. New York no longer spreads its infinity. The murmur of the city dissolves into a squall whose chill and power I no longer feel.'[1]

I don't particularly recall the density of the air changing when I was up the crane on my first visit to Dubai (and slightly higher than the World Trade Center), but I really know what he means when, walking to the end of the arm, you have the sensation of there being no higher to go. The beauty of that is there is nothing else; it is literally just you in that moment, and the world is very distant, very far below. And that's it, that's all there is – which is something that's a lot simpler than most people expect to hear. You just forget everything else . . .

1   Philippe Petit, *To Reach the Clouds*, Faber & Faber Ltd., 2002.

THE WORLD IS VERY DISTANT, VERY FAR BELOW

You really need to be up there yourself to experience it fully – then you'll nod, and say, 'Oh, I get it.' I don't really have the words for it. The main form of expression that I have is creating the videos. I'm not really expressing myself if no one is watching, right? The film-making is intimately tied up with what I do; the films have to be perfect, the music and the quality of the editing, everything. That's my form of self-expression. It's about doing something really well – the climbing and the representation of it all. That's my thing. It's all I've got, really: creating stuff, the videos. The whole thing is my work of art, I suppose.

I'm not really a people person, if I'm honest. I've never had much trouble being on my own. There are only a few people that I do really like and enjoy spending time with, and trust to that level. There's a lot of trust with the kind of stuff I'm involved in. If you're up high with someone and you don't trust them or you don't know how comfortable they are, how capable they are, it's weird – they're in your mind, but your mind needs to be clear in those situations. So if that's clouding my mind then that's a worry – and I don't really need that. I'll hang out with mates after a job or a shoot is done, but on the whole I surround myself with people I can totally trust.

I SURROUND MYSELF WITH PEOPLE I CAN TOTALLY TRUST

YOU CAN ALWAYS GO HIGHER

On a second trip to Dubai in 2015, my cousin Dave was on board as my manager and my friend Stevy flew out too. One night we were walking past the Almas Tower. There was no crane in sight, the building was finished and was topped by a distinct spire, which caught our attention. 'You should do that one,' said Dave. We scoped it out but there was security everywhere and loads of cameras – but maybe too many for someone to be watching all of them at once. We decided to return in the evening.

Later, the building was much quieter, and fairly open – it seemed to house mostly offices. We walked straight in, pretending to be normal tourists staying there. As we walked past, the guy behind the security desk didn't even raise his head. The cleaners had jammed open some doors with their buckets and Hoovers, so we walked into a 'staff only' area and found the fire-escape stairs, ran up those and discovered a new, separate lift system that you didn't need a card to operate. The lifts went up a certain number of levels –

to, say, the 47th floor – then we'd have to get out, cross the lobby and take the lift opposite up to the 64th floor, then out again, dart back across the corridor, and into another lift up the next section, and so on, to as far as we could go.

At such a height it could take a while for a lift to arrive, so some of the floors where we had to switch lifts had a sort of lounge area, with comfortable chairs where you could rest and enjoy the great view from the window. We were chillin'

in some of these chairs when we heard the lift go 'ding dong' and the doors flew open. That made us jump: 'Fuck, what's going on?' We froze in our lounge chairs. A guy walked from one lift to another, just a couple of metres from where we were sitting, but he seemed completely oblivious to us.

The lifts stopped before the top, and some stairs led us to where it seemed, eventually, we had reached the bottom of the spire. Over time you develop a second sense of where the right ladder will be. You can always go higher. We found that ladder – and then another ladder – in fact, ladder after ladder up inside a tapering conical shape. A bit like with the lift system, you'd get to the top of one ladder, then have to hop up, or over, onto another ladder – the space between the ladder and the wall narrowed each time. Pretty soon there was a decreasing sense of room and an increasing sense of claustrophobia. And all the time it was getting hotter and more airless – and we had no water. Those fucking ladders seemed to go up as far as the eye could see. It was getting late and we didn't know when or where those ladders would end – it felt like we might be climbing them for the rest of our lives. Forever trudging upwards, rung after rung, into a tapering steel cone.

We called it a night then decided to come back another evening, properly prepared.

And so a couple of nights later we were back. Despite once again strolling into the lobby with the ease of practised jet-setters, Dave decided that this time his role was to keep an eye on the street outside. 'You guys go on,' he gestured to me and Stevy, and so we just retraced our steps from a few nights earlier. This time we had cameras and plenty of water because of the heat.

It was much later than before, in the early hours of the morning, and on the stairs up to the service lifts we had to pick our way over plenty of Indian workers sleeping in stairwells, where it was much cooler. They were either workers or homeless people – one of them was just resting his head on a step, using it as a pillow.

Once again we were back at the foot of those ladders. This time we noticed a few air-conditioning units – air conditioning for the rest of the tower, that was. In our confined space they just hummed and pumped out heat and dust and shit. There was the odd dead bird for company too, and the lighting was dimmed. It wasn't particularly easy to breathe. Rung after rung, sweat was dripping off our arms and heads, splashing onto the dust. Onwards and upwards we climbed those convex-shaped ladders, the space getting tighter and tighter, the bag catching on everything. It must have been 50 degrees or more in there.

Then suddenly, at the top of a ladder, there was a heavy door. We shoved it open and there was an explosion of air; an inrushing blast, a bit like someone opening the passenger door on a jumbo jet over the Atlantic. It was so windy, so nice. On the film footage you can hear me groan, 'Ah, life . . .' We'd reached the halfway point of the spire, before it tapers to an even thinner needle at the top. You could see the marina at dawn, other towers still lit up; the amber strip of the E11 highway.

Then, roughly 380 metres up the Almas Tower, I felt the overwhelming call of nature and had to wipe my backside with a plastic bag we had on us. Later on in the film footage you can hear me complaining about the stink inside the spire, before Stevy points out, 'That's because you had a shit.'

We got back in the spire. There were, inevitably, a few more ladders. We came across another dead sparrow. The lighting wasn't great in there at all, and we were surprised when we suddenly hit the very tip-top. There was a tiny roof up there, enough space for one of us to stand in front of the hatch. The view was just awesome. I could make out the illuminated island in the Gulf where they're building Dubai's version of the London Eye – five times the size of the original model. We were 420 metres up, a bit lower than the crane, but with an incomparable view of the Dubai skyline. You could see the Cayan Tower, the famous twisted block of reinforced concrete, as well as the crane I'd been up a few months earlier. The air was fresh, the sun was just coming up, and I was fantasising about swooping down and hopping across the helipads and the flat tops of buildings. I love Dubai; I love the architecture – there's so much high stuff, and you can do pretty much what you want. It's a cool place, it's laid-back. The people are nice, there are no locks on half the doors. The morning was dead clear, there was a beautiful azure emptiness; in fact, it was unusually bright. We chilled around up there until the sun began to dim slightly, and what looked like a nasty sandstorm started to sweep in.

On the way back down we noticed another door we'd completely missed before. It led out onto the slanted roof that's a defining feature of the top of the tower when viewed in profile – the slope down from the bottom of the spire. Stevy filmed me doing a controlled slide down a drainage channel in the sloping roof, for about 30 or 40 metres. It was a bit like going down a water chute in Center Parcs, just with a 350-metre drop over the edge if you hit the bottom too fast – so it was definitely a controlled slide.

By this point the sandy haze was beginning to block out the marina. Even though it was still early in the morning the air became unpleasantly humid and a sandstorm out of nowhere pretty much enveloped us. That felt like the closest I've come to being shrouded in cloud – on a building, at least. It was so dry, hot and humid; the sand felt like dry paper. Pretty soon we couldn't see that far at all – we could just make out the halo of the sun. We came down. That storm lasted four days in all.

• • •

You can see me working out in the garden at Romsey in the Channel 4 film, swinging from the bars in the trees, going nuts; unseen by motorists flying by just the other side of the hedge. Mum and her partner Ian sorted out a digger to cement the scaffolding into the ground, and I bolted several bars through trees. For years I worked out there. The bars are good for balancing at high levels – if you lose your balance, you can always grab onto a tree. I'd get good at walking across one bar, then I'd build a higher bar, which was a bit scarier – then I'd master that, then another higher one, until I overcame the fear in my head and was walking backwards and forwards, over and over again, along bars 20 feet in the air as if I were strolling down Southampton High Street. I had floodlights out there too, and speakers wired up in the trees, pumping out Blink-182 (my childhood).

Prior to the trip to the Ukraine I was leaping about up there constantly. Today, I'm more likely to be on the roof of Burger King. All my apparatus in the garden is covered in leaves, and there are beetles living under the crash mats. I've outgrown it: because I'm so big and heavy, the scaffolding bars can move when I'm swinging on them and that kills all your momentum. When I buy my own house, I'll fill it with bars and fun stuff – I'll re-create my garden set-up indoors.

Mum says she still wakes up in the night – especially when somebody phones at 7:15 a.m. and she knows I'm out. She's still wired, waiting for something to happen. The last time the phone rang at a quarter-past seven in the morning she went into meltdown. It turned out to be some little old man who wanted a bit of work doing by my stepdad, Ian. She was literally shaking when she picked up the phone. It's been something of a traumatic journey for her. And even now Danny, my brother, will occasionally pop his head in the kitchen and say, 'Oh, James has been arrested in Dubai.' (The problem with Danny is that he worries about everything, and he makes things sound a hundred times worse than they actually are.) The police might get a report of someone acting suspiciously on a rooftop somewhere in town, and they'll phone up in the middle of the night: 'Is James in?'

Mum generally prefers the winter-time, when it's too wet and cold and dark for me to be up a crane. She can breathe easy then.

If anything, though, my off-the-road climbs have eased up in the last couple of years. Mum is not so freaked out by some of the professional jobs I take on – they're much safer. I did the Wembley arch wearing safety gear and a harness; it would have been too risky for the TV production company otherwise.

Personally, I hate all the safety gear: it's super-restrictive, I'm always snagging a bag or a harness on things; you can't lift your arm fully and you can't get your legs past a certain point. Recently I was hanging off the side of the tallest building in downtown Cape Town, the Southern Sun building, in a full rig – a strapped harness coming out of the back of my neck as I dangled off a bar at the top of the massive hotel. That was for a Wrangler advert. Still, I've learnt a lot about TV over the past few years. I like the creative process of shooting, editing and creating a final film for other people to enjoy – that's just awesome – but I'll never go super-official. Obviously, I need to get paid and everything, but I'll always remember where I came from. I do this stuff because I love it, and that's why I did it in the first place and why I continue to do it now. I don't do it for money, but I'm now in the comfortable position where I

get paid to do what I love. Even now I still don't like planning – I prefer the idea of not knowing what's coming next. But you can't really live like that when other people are involved . . . jobs like Wembley have to be planned.

Still, there are plenty of days when I'm fortunate enough to be able to wake up and be free to do whatever I want: travel round, have a blitz in the car. I've moved on from being addicted to conquering fear – I don't really have the fear any more, it's all gone. So what's next? Where does it go from here? I haven't really got a to-do list, as such. I've never been one to have goals and then go out to achieve them. Generally I take things as they come – just like the Eiffel Tower. I knew it was a possible climb, but we didn't have tickets booked and a schedule written – we just rocked up in Paris and ended up doing it. Wherever I am I still walk around with an eye on the skyline. There's a new bridge near Bristol, another in Scotland. Loads of stuff in London, Hong Kong, Toronto . . . there's a community of climbers out there. I still like the gritty, run-down urban stuff. You don't really get half-built concrete structures lying around, all exposed beams and frames, in the UK any more.

I HATE ALL THE SAFETY GEAR: IT'S SUPER-RESTRICTIVE

My mates on that first crane hang above Ocean Village in Southampton – Gibbs and Doug – now live together in Southampton but I haven't seen them for a while. I'm so lucky to get paid to do whatever I want, and I don't have to wake up at seven every morning and go to work just to pay the bills – but everybody else I know does. I can't just phone up a friend and say, 'Do you want to come to Dubai tomorrow?' because nobody can. Firstly, they've got jobs to go to; and secondly, it's not cheap to visit Dubai for two weeks. So that's another reason why I do stuff on my own. But I like it. Nowadays the only times I feel a bit down are usually to do with other people, and if I'm feeling a bit low then the best thing is to be on my own and just disconnect from everyone for a day or two. Then I can bring myself back up.

But at the top of a crane you leave shit to do with other people behind. You're up there and you look down, and you see all these tiny humans and their cars, all going to work – all the traffic, all the stress. Look at us: we're this massive planet, and we're getting stressed about our stupid little jobs and the system. When you're up high, you look down and you see how small we all are – how irrelevant we are. And yet we think we're everything, don't we? But we're all just grains of sand on the universe's beach – I like that analogy.

But then the top of the crane isn't really a place for negative thought. You're so focused on what you're doing up there,

in the here and now, that you forget everything else. I'm usually tired and covered in shit, but it's peaceful. It feels like nothing else exists, except for the faint city noise from below.

In his book *Skyfaring*, the 747 pilot Mark Vanhoenacker writes of how it is so much easier to deal with a queue in a bank or a traffic jam when you know that, in a few hours' time, you'll be flying over Greenland, or Nova Scotia, on your way to somewhere like California. He describes how it releases the mind and how, when you look down on cities from the cockpit, you can see it is all connected, 'how the patterns of streets, forests, suburbs, schools and rivers . . . the ordinary things we thought we knew become new or more beautiful, and the visible relationships between them on land, particularly at night, hint at the circuitry of more or less everything.' [2]

For me, that's best captured in Dubai in the middle of the night: all the street lights are on, everything is illuminated, super-well lit. There are massive freeways that spin and flip over each other – you don't really notice them until night-time. I think I've caught all that detail in the film and in the photographs – well, at least until the sandstorm came in, and all you could see was the halo of the sun.

2   Mark Vanhoenacker, *Skyfaring: A Journey with a Pilot*, Vintage/Penguin Random House, 2015.